Panther Chamele

Panther Chameleon Owne

Panther Chameleon book for care, feeding, handling, health and common myths.

by

Jonathan Durham

Table of Contents

Introduction

The word Chameleon comes from the Greek words "Chamai" and "Leon" meaning 'Earth Lion.'

These creatures originate from the lizard family and in their natural habitat tend to live in trees, although some species can also be found in low shrubs and scrubs.

Chameleons are unusual because they can change the colour of their skin, a fact most people know even if they've never seen one in real life. This, along with their beautiful colours and patterns and interesting behaviour, have made chameleons more popular in recent years and they are now some of the most sought after reptiles.

This book focuses on the Panther Chameleon, so called not because it looks anything like a panther but because of its aggressive nature.

Chapter 1: The Panther Chameleon

Introduction

The Panther chameleon is one of the most popular chameleons to keep as a pet. Although it ought to be said that no chameleon is particularly easy to keep, some are more suited to captivity than others and the Panther chameleon is one of these, assuming that all its needs are met.

Whilst they originally occurred only in Madagascar, they have now been successfully introduced to Mauritius and the island of La Réunion and studies seem to show that these types of chameleons don't really have a preference for any particular habitat, which could be one reason why they adapt to captivity.

The Panther chameleons have different names depending on the location in which they are found, so the Nosy Be Panther Chameleon is found on the island of Nosy Be, the Andapa Panther Chameleon is from the neighboring island of Andapa and so on. There are a few exceptions to this rule such as the Picasso or the Mafana, which have been given 'designer' names either because the exporter doesn't want to reveal which location these particular creatures originated from or so that a higher price tag can be attached by selling them as designer and therefore special. Whilst their features are generally the same – the differing names aren't indicative of a separate species or subspecies - male Panther chameleons will have slightly different coloring depending on their region.

It can take several months for a baby Panther chameleon to show any colors but for adults, their colors and patterns are often the most vibrant of any chameleon species. The males can have bright blue-green, emerald-green, light green or turquoise bodies with bands or splashes of white, yellow, purple or black. Even their lips can be bright yellow or white and their eye turrets may have gold, red or orange around them depending on their geographical location. The females tend to stay peach, pink, tan or brown although they may have spots of turquoise or blue.

Although these are thought to be one of the most docile breeds of chameleons, they are still territorial and are solitary animals, even in the wild.

Size
Male Panther chameleons are typically around 12-18 inches in total length, including their tail, although some have been seen to reach up to 20-22 inches in length. Females are typically smaller and are usually only around 10-14 inches including their tail. Again it depends on their breed and location.

However you still need to have a fairly large cage for both male and female Panther chameleons, so before buying assess whether you have room for it. The upshot of owning a Panther chameleon is that they like to climb, therefore your cage needs to be vertical rather than horizontal so unlike a fish tank that tends to take up a whole wall, your chameleon cage will need to be tall, taking space that would not necessarily be used otherwise.

Lifespan
Panther chameleons tend to have shorter life spans compared to other breeds of chameleons. In captivity, males can live approximately four to seven years. On average, females tend to live about half as long as males, usually about two to three years due to the toll egg laying can take on their bodies. If owners help the females to lay fewer eggs, then this can increase their life span.
Of course this longevity depends on how well you take care of them and cater for their specific needs. Some owners report that their chameleons have lived far longer than this, whereas others only have

6

them for six months to a year. You need to research thoroughly before you even think about purchasing one.

Like humans, chameleons can get noticeably more delicate as they get older and are more susceptible to illness and injury so it is important to monitor your chameleon to try and spot illness and injury early enough to be treated.

Interesting Features

Part of why the chameleon is so interesting is because of its amazing characteristics that make it unique.

Eyes

A chameleon's eyes are globe shaped and protrude from their head. For a reptile, the chameleon has great eyesight and can see small insects from fairly long distances but what makes them particularly special is that they can swivel their eyes independently from each other, meaning the chameleon can look both behind and in front at the same time. When searching for food, a chameleon will often move both eyes in different directions until it finds a target. Once this has been spotted, the clever creature will usually focus both eyes on the prey in order to judge the distance and its aim. Another advantage of these amazing eyes is that the chameleon can keep one eye on its prey whilst it creeps towards it yet also be on the lookout for predators.

Projectile Tongue

This is one of the chameleon's most remarkable adaptations. Approximately twice the length of its body, the tongue is hollow with a large, sticky tip. Scientists have discovered that the tongue works a bit like a catapult. When the chameleon sees its prey, a contracting muscle will shoot its tongue out at lightning speed. The prey will get trapped on the sticky pad and then crushed to prevent escape. A different muscle then draws the tongue back up into the mouth where it's bunched up like an accordion until it's needed again.

To see this in action, place food at different distances and watch the chameleon snap it up. It takes around 0.07 seconds and they have around a ninety percent success rate, so if you blink you'll miss it!

Legs And Feet

These are unique because their toes are fused together, giving them a pincer look. Each foot has three toes opposing two toes, which work in a similar way that our opposing thumb and other fingers do. On the front they have the three toes on the inside and the two on the outside, whereas the back feet are the opposite. The sharp claws on the end and the small, rough scales beneath enable the chameleon to grip onto twigs, making them expert climbers.

Gait

This is slow and deliberate and is thought to be part of the chameleon's strategy of escaping unnoticed and aiding it to camouflage itself. Sometimes you may see them rocking back and forth as they move, giving the effect of a leaf moving in the breeze. This illusion is aided by the creature's flattened sides, enabling it to hide in the tree branches. If necessary, chameleons are capable of running quickly for short distances but they shouldn't need to do this very often in captivity.

Tail

This is prehensile, meaning it has evolved to grasp and acts almost as a fifth foot by twisting and twining itself around branches, enabling the chameleon to secure itself in the trees.

Color

Caused by special cells, this is probably the chameleon's most famous characteristic, yet it is also misunderstood. Who hasn't seen a cartoon or a TV program depicting a chameleon changing color so dramatically on any background, plain or patterned, that all you can see are its eyes? Sorry to disappoint you but placing your new pet on tartan material won't cause it to appear checked nor is it solely for camouflage. In fact the ability to mimic its background color is limited to lighter or darker coloration and it is affected more by temperature or mood.

When the chameleon is cold it will usually darken, as this attracts the heat, and when it is warm it will turn a lighter shade in order to reflect the heat away from its body.

Color changes are also used to communicate, showing whether the animal is angry or scared or used in territorial displays to depict who is the more dominant. With two males confronting one another these changes can be dramatic – becoming suddenly brighter and color patterns that were previously hidden or insignificant may appear as vivid stripes, blotches and spots. The brighter the colors, the more dominant the male is and in any of these territorial displays the brighter color male almost always wins. A submissive male often turns brown or grey.

Females also use color to accept or reject a suitor or to indicate that she's already pregnant.

Life Cycle Of A Chameleon

There are four basic life stages for chameleons and it is important to understand each stage in order to become a successful Herpetoculturist. These are:

1. Pre-birth/Embryonic
2. Juvenile/Sub-adult
3. Sexually Mature Adult
4. Old Age

Let's look at each in turn.

Pre-Birth/Embryonic

This should only really concern you if you are a breeder of chameleons and owners should not need to worry about this stage at all. However it's included here in case you wish to breed your chameleons and also as it's the beginning of the life cycle. Breeders should understand and practice proper management including ensuring the female chameleons are provided with good nutrition and that the incubation conditions are suitable as both of these factors will impact the egg and embryonic development.

Juvenile/Sub-adult

This is characterized by the small size of the creature followed by rapid growth. At this stage the chameleon's main priority is to grow, which means they will mainly be concerned with food. As an owner you should provide them with as much food as they can eat but of course ensure they are getting a varied and nutritional diet.

Aggression amongst others of its own kind and territorial behaviors won't yet be an issue, so it is possible to keep more than one in an enclosure, which is good news for those breeders that find they have sixty or more eggs hatching in one go. However, any larger animals will have a competitive advantage of the smaller ones and will eventually end up intimidating them, which will cause stress to both creatures, so this arrangement shouldn't be indefinite. Please don't make the mistake that a lot of owners do in believing that because two eggs hatched at the same time and the chameleons were kept in the same enclosure as babies they can continue living this way for the rest of their lives because it just isn't true. One will always dominate the other, significantly reducing the life span of both.

Sexually Mature Adult

By this stage they will have reached a size where they can successfully reproduce, therefore growth rate slows because their body now focuses its energy resources on reproduction rather than growth, particularly with females. Owners need to be aware of this change because excessive feeding at this stage can cause obesity in both sexes and can lead the females to overproduce eggs. This is the stage where you need to monitor and reduce food intake and supplementation and possibly lower the temperature slightly for female chameleons. Remember that even if you're not breeding your female, if you can reduce the number of clutches she has per year and the amount of eggs in each clutch, then her life span can be greatly lengthened.

This is also the time where these creatures become territorial and show aggressive and defensive displays as well as developing aggressive behavior. Any chameleons previously housed together need to be separated and kept out of sight of each other.

Old Age

Sadly many chameleons in captivity won't reach this life stage at all. If it is attained it is characterized by infrequent (if any) egg production, reduced feeding and limited activity.
To extend the chameleon's life span at this age, owners should reduce the amount of food they provide as well as reducing the calories in their diet by providing less treats.

Although some people don't concern themselves with the life stages of the chameleon I think that it's helpful for a good owner and/or breeder to understand each one in order to monitor their animal(s) and make adjustments to their feeding schedule and their chameleon's environment in order to successfully accommodate the changes each life stage brings. This can greatly extend the life of the captive chameleon.

Chapter 2: Before You Buy

You may have your heart set on an exotic pet, maybe you've seen a chameleon on television and heard that a Panther Chameleon is a hardier species and therefore is the best one to choose. Before you go running off to the pet store there are a few things you need to know in order to decide whether or not a Panther Chameleon is suitable for you.

Is A Panther Chameleon For Me?

Do panther chameleons make good pets? The simple answer to this is yes! They are beautiful, fascinating creatures and if you like reptiles then they can be excellent pets.

However it does depend on what you are looking for in a pet; if you want an animal that you can take out and play with or teach tricks to then this creature is definitely not for you. They're not companion animals like cats and dogs, in fact they're not very sociable at all and although many people say that a Panther Ccameleon is friendlier than other breeds of chameleons it will never be a companion animal and handling should be kept to a minimum because it can cause them a lot of stress. Think of them as more of a "look and observe" creature like fish, rather than a playful one. For this reason they are not particularly suitable for young children or those who want something they can touch and pick up and play with all the time.

All chameleons are very high maintenance and they are not something to be purchased on impulse, as they require a great deal of resources and dedication. Although the Panther chameleon does appear to be able to tolerate temperature changes and seem to adapt to captivity, they are not recommended for novices and if you've never owned a reptile before it is advised you choose something else first like a Corn Snake, Bearded Dragon or a Gecko until you have more experience. Having said that, they're not the most difficult exotic creature to keep and as long as you do your research so that you know what to expect and how to care for them properly you can raise these creatures successfully.

Panther chameleons are better alone, as they are very territorial and although you can keep a male and a female together for breeding purposes, once they've been bred the pair should always be separated again. Two males together is a definite no-no. Even being kept in separate cages can cause them to display aggressive behavior if they can see each other, which can cause unnecessary stress and lead to injury. Females are less territorial but it is recommended that you only ever keep one of these creatures at any one time. If this seems cruel then remember that they are solitary and territorial creatures and even in the wild it is very rare that two males (or females for that matter) would voluntarily remain within sight of each other.

Some households are inappropriate for these creatures for instance those with children under five, pregnant women, those with a compromised immune system or elderly people shouldn't be keeping this type of pet. Partly because of the risk of disease transmission but also because they need a quiet household as well as a dedicated owner willing to spend a lot of time to take care of them.

So why are they so difficult?
In captivity a lot of Panther chameleons don't live past eighteen months. To raise them successfully you need to understand how they live in the wild. They spend most of their time in treetops, soaking up direct sunlight and eating a wide variety of insects and occasional plants.

Three of the biggest challenges are to ensure a full spectrum of lighting, warm temperatures and a good mixture of suitable insects.

You may read that the Panther chameleon is the hardiest and the easiest type of chameleon to breed and look after. Whilst this can be true, the problem is that if they are purchased on a whim without the necessary equipment they will not live very long. They need a specialist environment as close to the conditions wild chameleons would experience, therefore you need to be prepared and do a lot of research on their care requirements.

For these reasons, whilst they are good for someone who is looking to buy their first chameleon they're not so good for a beginner reptile keeper.

Cost To Purchase

Okay, I hope you're sitting down for this one. A Panther chameleon is one of the most expensive breeds and in the UK can cost anywhere between £125 to £425 depending on its age and locale so an Ambilobe or Nosy Be tend to be slightly cheaper than the Nosy Faly for instance. In America they will cost anywhere between $200 to $600.

The cost is also dependent upon where you buy it from: online prices, for instance, are more expensive than a pet shop. Now you may be saying, okay they're pricy but so are pedigree dogs and if you save up then you can afford it, after all they are exotic animals. However that is just the cost of buying one. Keeping it is a different story.

Set-up requires a large cage, the larger the better, add in the plants, lighting and heating and it can be a costly affair. Then you have food plus any items that need to be replaced after six months or so such as the light bulbs.

The following is a rough estimate of the cost of setting up and keeping a Panther chameleon. (Please note prices were correct at the time of going to press-, although these can change according to currency fluctuations, which, of course are out of the author's control).

Set Up Costs
Panther Chameleon - £125-425+ ($200-600)
Vivarium - £210+   ($279)
Plants - £50-£100+ ($81-135) (depending on if they're artificial or real)
Substrate - £5-10 ($6-14)

Lighting
UVB light bulb £18.99+ ($25+)
Light fixtures and stands - £70+ ($94+)
Basking Lamp - £29.99+ ($40+)
Basking light bulbs £15.49 (Pack of two) ($21+)
Reflector - £8.79+ ($12+)
Timer for Lights - £6.99+ ($9+)
Digital Hygrometer for temperature and humidity - £6.79+ ($9+)
Heat Guard - £10.69+ ($14.50+)

Watering
Hand spray bottle £1.99+ ($2.70+)
Drippers (basic) £7.99+ ($10.82+)
Automatic Mister £39.99+ ($54.16+)

Food (Approximately a month's worth)

Baby Chameleon:
Flightless Fruit Flies - £3.83 ($5.19)
Small crickets £2.81 ($3.81)
Mini mealworms £8.95 ($12.12)

Adult Chameleon:
Crickets - £2.81 ($3.81)
Waxworms - £2.45($3.32)
Mealworms - £8.95 ($12.12)
Butterworms - £6.60 ($8.94)
Dubia Roaches - £3.50 ($4.74)
Locusts - £4.20 ($5.69)

Containers for insects - £11.99 each ($16.24)
Cost to gut-load food – Approx. £20+ per month ($27+)

Supplements
Phosphorous Free Calcium With Vitamin D3 - £8.19 ($11.09)
Phosphorous Free Calcium Without Vitamin D3 - £7.05 ($9.60)

Vet Bills
Dependent on area - £15+ consultation ($20+)
Operations or medicines - £30+ ($40+)

Let's say I buy a Panther chameleon for around £200 ($264). We'll
go with a middle range – I wouldn't recommend buying a really
cheap one because I would be suspicious of health conditions
although sometimes new or inexperienced breeders may sell cheap
because their female has produced a large clutch and they need to
sell them off before they reach an age where they can't be housed
together anymore) so this is the price I found on a reputable breeders
site. If I then add everything on the above list spending £60 on plants
and choosing an automatic mister instead of an ordinary hand spray
bottle then it would come to around £754.46 ($1002.22). This is
without an egg laying bin or any containers to keep my insects in. If
I decided to buy 6 insect containers at £11.99 then this would come
to another £71.94 making a grand total of £826.40 (around $1097).
Yes, I could make this slightly cheaper by taking off the automatic
mister and using a hand spray bottle and using margarine tubs

instead of insect containers and I probably don't need a lights timer but if we're looking at the optimal set up this is about the cheapest you could do it for. Bear in mind that the £210 is for the smallest cage you could possibly keep your Panther chameleon in. Ideally you would want the tallest possible cage, which could put you out around £300 (close to $400 in the US). Plus, if you're buying from pet shops or breeders rather than over the Internet, your prices could be slightly increased again.

The cost of gut loading food is based on if you have around four different types of insects and you spend a pound a week on vegetables and fruit for gut loading – this could be more or less dependent on where you shop and the prices in your area. Lighting costs will vary depending on how you set them up but all in all, realistically, you're looking at a minimum of £826 to set up and buy your Panther chameleon.

With regards to cost I would give you three pieces of advice:

1. If you really have your heart set on one of these beautiful creatures then you should buy a little bit of equipment each week or month (depending on what you can afford) and set everything up over time. Not only does this spread the cost but it also gives you time to research the perfect environment and husbandry techniques. I do feel that if you are putting in a time commitment and buying things a little bit here and there that you are also serious about owning one rather than buying on a whim.

2. My second piece of advice would be to price up what it costs to insure your Panther chameleon. Yes, they may never get sick and it might not be worth your while but if you're a novice owner there is a higher chance your chameleon could become ill and you would need to see the vet (preferably one that specializes in exotic animals, particularly chameleons)

and these visits aren't often cheap, especially if they prescribe medication or say your pet needs an operation. It may not be worthwhile doing but I do think it's worth researching.

3. The third piece of advice would be to maybe look at reducing your food costs by raising your own insect colonies. This may not be an option for you if you are squeamish – although let's get this straight now, your Panther chameleon NEEDS live insects to stay healthy. Some people don't like the noises the crickets and some other insects make but if you're going to be keeping Panther chameleons then it could be a good idea.

Breeding kits range from around £9.50 - £17.99 (approximately $12-24) upwards depending on what type of insects you're breeding and where you buy them. You can buy a variety of kits such as crickets, mealworms, wax worms, locusts and so on. Don't forget you will need to feed these animals as well, so your cost of gut loading will increase and you will need to maintain these insects properly, such as cleaning out their containers and replenishing their food daily, removing any insects that have died and so on. It isn't for everyone but is something worth thinking about.

Where To Buy

There are a lot of choices and they all have advantages and disadvantages, so I'm not going to recommend one over the other. There are good and bad pet shops just as there are good and bad breeders and good and bad owners. Whichever method you choose is entirely up to you but with a bit of information you should be able to make your own mind up about whether the person is reputable or not.

I will say this – never be pressured into buying and never buy a chameleon because you feel sorry for it or because you are so excited and desperate to own one. If you end up buying one that has been mistreated or is already ill then chances are no matter how perfect your set up is, it will die.

The following are the main options for buying:

Pet Shop

I hear a lot of people saying these are a no-no when it comes to exotic pets, especially chameleons. Yes, there may be pet shops that stock these creatures without knowing how to care for them. I've never been to a pet shop that only has one sort of pet with each one kept in separate cages where they can't see each other; this being a major requirement for a chameleon. However, I can't tar all pet shops with the same brush. Some are specialists in exotic pets and these are the best ones to go to. Usually they're small and local rather than big chains so may be slightly more expensive, but the advantages of buying from them are that you can talk to people and ask their advice about the animal and the vivarium. A good pet shop will know a lot about the creatures and will be able to answer pretty much every question you have. Usually they'll be enthusiastic and willing to talk to you and share their knowledge and experience.

Another advantage is if you are sold a sick chameleon you have somebody to hold accountable, as you can return to a pet shop or put in a complaint. You can also see the chameleon in person, where and how it's been kept and check its health before you buy. You can also ask about its feeding habits, age, sex and where it was sourced from.

The disadvantage is that pet shops, no matter how good they are, aren't ideal environments for chameleons and they may be sick purely because of the conditions they are kept in. The owners or workers may be keener on making money than they are about the creature's well being and they may try and sell you a whole load of things that aren't suitable or even necessary.

The best way to avoid this is to do your research so you know what to be alert for and to know the right questions to ask and what the right answers should be.

Reptile Fair
These are great, as you will have both pet shops and breeders available and there will be so many creatures to choose from. However, in this setting it's not possible to see how they have been raised or housed.

The good news is you will be able to talk to people directly and ask about their experience with exotic pets. Usually the people attending these types of fairs are very knowledgeable and again you will be able to check the health of the Panther chameleons for yourself. Always ask for the contact information of a seller so you can ask questions later if you need to and again, so that you have someone to hold accountable should anything go wrong.

The downside of these fairs is that the person you buy from will usually live far away so it's not feasible to go there for advice or to buy supplies once you have purchased your Panther chameleon.

Breeder
I said I wasn't going to recommend a particular option but this is by far my favorite. You read and research and then you book an appointment with a professional breeder with a reputation for producing healthy animals. If you're searching online then by all means check any reviews that have been posted to see what other people think but be aware that these aren't always trustworthy – most people will only post a review if they've had a bad experience

and of course people known to the breeder could post false reviews to make them look good.

The reason why this is one of the best options is you can see how the chameleons have been raised and kept. You can ask questions and get an idea of whether the breeder is being honest with you as well as how knowledgeable and experienced they are.

If you don't like the set up or the look of the chameleons then you don't buy, but usually this isn't the case, as in order to have a good reputation as a breeder you usually have to be an expert in keeping these creatures healthy in order to hatch the eggs successfully and keep the offspring alive for the first three months before you sell them. If a breeder is inviting you into their home, they're most likely proud of their set up and willing for you to inspect it. Not only that, but a responsible breeder may interrogate you as to your set up and knowledge of these creatures. Don't be offended if this happens, instead see it as a good sign – clearly if they're worried about the type of home the babies are going to then they love these creatures and aren't in it just for money.

The advice of these breeders is gold – they can tell you the brands of the lamps they use, where they buy their supplies, the type of calcium supplement and food the chameleons have been eating and even how often they eat and poop. As these chameleons are being raised as pets, they will most likely have handled them from a young age and will be able to show you how to do this properly. They may also have an idea of each one's temperament, so if you do want a 'friendly' one now would be the time to ask. (But be prepared for the breeder to say never handle them at all).

You still need to do your homework and don't just rely on the information purely from one owner, but if you do this before visiting you should be pretty confident about whether or not the breeder is trustworthy and safe to buy from. Of course the downside to buying from breeders is that you may have to travel quite far in order to visit, which means you may be more tempted to buy there and then. If this is the case, please ensure your set up is prepared at home before you visit the breeders.

Private Seller
Unlike a breeder who is raising chameleons from birth in order to sell them on, private sellers are mostly people who have bought a Panther chameleon but are selling it on because they can't – or won't – take care of them.

These can be healthy and properly cared for but you need to ask yourself why is this person selling? It may be that they have purchased the chameleon and then realized, too late, the amount of work it involves and have realized they don't have the time or the expertise to care for it. It may be because they are moving away and can't take it with them for whatever reason or maybe they've changed jobs and know they won't have as much time for it.

However, there are also those people that have realized that the chameleon isn't healthy, possibly because they lack understanding of how to care for it properly. Sorry if I sound condescending here but let's face it, it's not fun taking care of a sick animal that needs pricy medical attention, so most people in this situation would want to sell it on as quickly as possible.

A responsible owner who wants a good home for their beloved pet will be willing to help you assess the health of the chameleon. They will have kept good records of its food, cage temperatures, humidity levels and health and should be willing to let you go to their house and check it out should you wish to do so.

A major advantage of buying this way is that the private seller may be selling the vivarium, lighting and all the other equipment that goes with it. You can find some good deals on the Internet for the whole set up from around £350 ($465).

The downside of this is that, again, an owner may be far from where you live. An owner may offer for you to visit them and then they will deliver it if you wish to buy it, giving them an opportunity to check out the living arrangements you will be providing the creature with. These would be the best type of people to buy from because again, they clearly love their pet enough to check out its potential new home.

Internet

This can be a private owner, pet shop or breeder shipping to you. It's by far the quickest and easiest option. You can read information from their websites, ask questions via email and see photographs. You don't have to travel far – or at all – and you can buy, pay and ship overnight.

I have to say that this, for me, is the worst possible way to buy any pet, especially a chameleon. You don't know where the exotic pet is coming from, how it's raised or housed or what its health is like and you're now also adding the trauma of shipping into the mix.

Your questions are being answered by a faceless, unknown person who could just be telling you what you want to hear and how do you even know the picture you have seen is of the chameleon you are buying? Who is held accountable if something goes wrong or you have a complaint?

Wherever you buy from always choose a captive-bred chameleon, as wild ones often carry parasites and diseases, which mean they may already be sick or getting sick by the time they reach you. These creatures are delicate enough and don't need the stress of being caught, plus they find it very difficult to adapt to captive conditions, which will make it even harder for you to keep them alive.

In many countries it is illegal to capture and transport wild chameleons, so by purchasing one you are supporting a trade where many animals die horrible, slow deaths before they even reach the pet store or new owner.

Instead, if you choose not to buy from a breeder directly, look for ethically-sourced chameleons; those that have been captive-bred and raised properly.

What To Look For

As chameleons are incredibly difficult to look after it is very important that you have a healthy one to start with. They should have a smooth, even body with no sign of mites. It is very difficult to assess if a chameleon is sick because they are wild animals and as such are adept at hiding illness or injury, as these would make them a target for predators in the wild.

Signs Of A Healthy Chameleon

- Full, smooth, rounded, even body.
- Strong, even, smooth jawline.
- Fat, rounded tail.

Always be sure to check the following:

Eyes – These should be clear and bright, bulging and turret-like in appearance, not cloudy or sunken and should be actively moving about as the lizard views its surroundings, especially as you approach it.

Mouth – Look for an irregular jawline or dents in the mouth with or without a cottage cheese-like substance known as mouth rot.

Body – If you can see the chameleon's ribs or hipbones protruding, it is most likely undernourished. Look for open wounds, bite marks, swollen toes or a limp, as these are indicators that the chameleon has been injured. Red, fluid-filled patches can indicate thermal burns. The chameleon's body should be brightly colored and not dull unless it's in shed, and although they are naturally slow creatures, they should still be active and have a good, strong grip on the branches and twigs.

Feces – Not the greatest thing to inspect but if there's any evidence of loose, unhealthy stools or there are feces smeared at the animal's anal opening then this is another sign that it could have a health condition.

Mites – These are reddish-brown spots around the mouth, eyes and ear area.

Questions To Ask

Is the chameleon wild caught or captive bred? – You should never buy a wild-caught chameleon. These often carry parasites and can have other medical issues. Not only that but they don't tend to live as long, as they find it difficult to adapt to captivity.

Can I see the animal's health records? - It is very important to keep a journal for each animal that records feeding, instances of refusing feeds, defecation, shredding and unusual behavior or changes in behavior along with the dates of bulb changes. This not only helps the owner to monitor their Panther chameleon and flag up any signs of ill health, but also helps the vet troubleshoot health issues.

When buying a chameleon you should ask to check these records, especially if you're buying a second hand pet.

When was the last physical examination? – This applies more to older chameleons, and again this is especially important from private sellers but it can also apply to younger chameleons and breeders. For an exotic pet like this they should have regular physical exams, at least once a year.

How old is the chameleon? – Avoid buying very young chameleons under three months old unless you are a very experienced keeper. Under three months and they're usually not ready to move to a new home, their feeding habits won't yet be established and it won't always be clear if they have any health defects or not.

How often is the chameleon handled? – If you are buying from a private seller or a pet shop, the answer could well be never. This is fine, after all chameleons don't enjoy being handled and I would never recommend you do this. They are a merely to be enjoyed by watching, after all you would never pull a tropical fish from a tank so why would you want to cuddle your chameleon? However, if you buy from a breeder who handles them from very young, the chameleons can get used to it. Having a chameleon you can pick up every now and then without causing too much stress can be handy if, for example, you want to take them outside, or you want to free range them for exercise, or if you need to take them to the vet.

What does the chameleon eat? – The answer to this will probably be crickets but if you ask what else they've been given it can give you an idea of its favorite treats as well as the feed it doesn't like. Knowing this can help you settle your chameleon quicker and is advantageous if you are trying to handle them, as you can offer something they enjoy. Chameleons should be given a variety of different foods, so this will help you determine whether they are being provided a healthy, nutritious diet – if you are buying an adult chameleon that only has a diet of crickets then this signals that they aren't getting a balanced diet and therefore may have health problems as a result of this.

What is the chameleon's temperament like? – Knowing this will give you an idea of whether you should handle the chameleon or not. If you are buying a laid back juvenile from a breeder that handles it every day then this gives an indication that you would be okay to handle it every now and then. If you are buying, say, an older chameleon or one that shows signs of stress whenever somebody comes near, then handling it will be a no-no, and if you are buying a chameleon you can take out and pet then this probably won't be suitable for you.

Why are you selling? – Of course this question is redundant if you're buying from a breeder or a pet shop as the reason is obvious – they want to make money, and in the case of breeders, they have too many chameleons and need to get rid of them. However, this is more for if you are buying a chameleon from a private seller, especially if they've only had them a short while.

Of course they may not tell you the truth – I doubt very much anyone would say "oh I haven't looked after it properly and it's going to cost me an extortionate amount in vet bills to make it healthy again" but hopefully if you speak over the telephone or, even better, in person, you will be able to get a measure of the person and decide whether they are being honest or not. If you meet in person you should also have the chance to examine the chameleon, see its habitat and get an idea of whether it's healthy or not.

If you are buying an older, second hand chameleon I would also recommend you ask how long the person has owned it. You may well be buying a two year old chameleon and assume that the person selling has had it since it was a baby and this may not necessarily be the case – maybe they purchased it from somebody else when it was eighteen months or a year old. I wouldn't recommend buying a Panther chameleon that has been passed from person to person, as you cannot determine what its life has been like or how it's been kept in each home.

Chapter 3: Male or Female

How To Identify The Sex

If you're a novice chameleon owner it's recommended that you try and buy a male rather than a female, as they are slightly hardier and you don't have the added complication of egg laying. Females tend to have a shorter lifespan because carrying and laying eggs, whether they have been bred or not, uses up a lot of energy and over the years can often take its toll on their bodies.

Sexing a Panther chameleon can be tough at first, although it is possible to do this when it has hatched straight from the egg.

Male Panther chameleons tend to be more popular because of their amazing array of colors and patterns, which the female of the species don't have. That isn't to say they aren't as fascinating, but many people (understandably so) are taken by the striking appearance of the males. I have heard numerous stories of pet shops selling female Panther chameleons as males and by the time the owners realize they've been duped it's too late. Therefore, although color can be an indication of sex, it is more appropriate when the chameleon is older as some males will stay tan or brown until six months of age when they become sexually mature.

So how do you distinguish a male from a female? I would advise you go on the Internet and search for different photographs of males and females. Ideally these pictures will be taken from the side with the chameleon's tail sticking out. (if you are a breeder or a selling a chameleon this pose is usually done by putting the chameleon on a ruler to walk along.)

Look at the back and tail of the chameleon. A male will have a straight line from its stomach down and along the tail. The base of the tail will be slightly thicker in order to accommodate its sexual organs when matured. A male Panther chameleon that is around three months upwards will have a bulge at the base of the tail, which is more obvious than when first born.

Females on the other hand will have an indentation near their back legs and their tail base will be much narrower. Their tails also tend to be thinner so they appear to have a gentler slope from the base of the tail to the end.

Males will also have a more prominent rostral process (the nasal ridge or bump on its 'nose'). This will grow outwards as they mature, whereas females only have a tiny rostral process.

Identifying a male or female isn't easy, as some males can be less obvious as they will have a tiny rostral process and small bulge, and some females may start to show a bit of color here, which can be misleading. Unless you are an expert you may have to rely on the information that is given to you by the person you are purchasing it from, so you need to decide whether or not you trust them.

If you are not sure whether you are buying a male or female and it really is important to you then my advice would be to wait and get an older chameleon that is around six months or older when their colors are showing. If you really don't mind then I would simply say trust the seller and just be prepared in case you have been sold a female instead of a male or vice versa. If you know you will love your chameleon anyway then it isn't really a problem as long as you introduce an egg-laying bin to a female's cage.

Female Egg Laying

Like chickens, female Panther chameleons will lay eggs whether they have mated or not. A common myth is that if a female chameleon is not mated then she will die egg bound. This is not true. She will produce and lay eggs 2-3 times a year regardless of whether she has been mated, however if she is not given a suitable place to lay the eggs then she can retain them. Retained eggs absorb the nutrients that a female Panther chameleon needs to survive and may even compress her lungs until she suffocates, so it is a serious problem. Egg retention is also referred to as being egg bound.

Keeping a female Panther chameleon at a slightly cooler temperature than you would a male and not over-feeding them can reduce the size of the clutches and the frequency at which she lays subsequent clutches, therefore in theory, lengthening her lifespan, although some females in captivity never produce a clutch at all.

Egg Laying Bin

This will need to be provided at around six months. To make a suitable egg laying bin use a plastic container as large as the space in the enclosure will allow but bear in mind that it must be big enough for your chameleon to fit into easily whilst still having space around her, including above and ideally at least ten to twelve inches in depth. A chameleon will dig down to the bottom, so the container shouldn't be shallow. If you don't provide her with a nesting site that she deems suitable she may find her own by digging into a plant pot – if they do this the eggs are usually eventually laid near the roots of the plant, so this should give you an idea of how deep they like to dig. The container should also be opaque rather than transparent to give her a sense of security.

Once you have found a suitable tub you will need to fill it with damp play sand or organic soil. (Don't use sand that contains lime such as builders' sand). Sometimes a mixture is better as although a soil base is more natural, some owners have reported that their female refuses to dig in soil but sand alone can be harder to dig through. Whatever you choose it should be damp enough to hold a tunnel but not soaking wet. Remember that it may take a few days and your sand/soil mixture can dry out, so you need to check it regularly and add more water if necessary.

Be aware that if you use an automatic mister or dripping system that you need to position your egg laying bin where it won't be flooded by these water sources. If it is too wet it makes digging far more difficult and not only is there a risk of your chameleon drowning but the eggs will also become ruined if they are wet. Whilst this may just be sad if they're infertile, if you've bred your chameleon and they are fertile eggs then obviously once ruined the baby chameleons won't be able to hatch.

Some female chameleons don't feel comfortable lying in a tub that only contains a substrate, so it might be a good idea to put a plant in the center to make your chameleon feel more secure.

What Happens Next?
Once your female starts digging it is very important that she is left alone. It is highly recommended that you cover the cage because if she sees you watching she'll think that the egg-laying site she has chosen is unsafe. She will abandon the tunnel she has started and try again elsewhere. If this happens too often the urge to lay will eventually pass and she may become egg bound. (See chapter nine for more information on this condition).

It can take a few days for her to find the right position and excavate a tunnel that she's satisfied with. Once this is done she will turn around and lay. How many eggs are laid within each clutch varies amongst females and can also depend on whether the clutches are fertile or not. Fertile clutches tend to produce fewer amounts but plumper eggs.

Infertile eggs are cream or yellow in color and similar in size to a jellybean or large baked bean. Fertile eggs tend to be whiter and slightly larger.

Once the female has finished laying her eggs she will fill the hole in order to cover the eggs. The soil or sand will be packed quite tightly and often you may struggle to see where she has been digging, which makes it difficult for you to find the eggs should you wish to dig them up.

When she has finished she will return to the branches. Often she will look dark, skinny and dehydrated. It is important that at this point you offer her a long misting session so she can drink and also give her food so she can regain her energy

What Happens If She Doesn't Lay Eggs?

If you think your female is due to lay eggs but you don't see her digging in her laying bin but scratching around elsewhere in her cage then it may be that she doesn't like the container you have provided. If this is the case then try to place her in another container such as a tall kitchen bin (obviously clean and bought for this purpose). Use a soil to sand mix and add a few small branches.

As female chameleons tend to lay closer to the evening, if you place her there mid-afternoon and leave her she should eventually lay. Try not to check on her too often – if you are worried you could always try setting up a webcam in order to keep an eye on her. If the room temperature is above 21C (70F) then you shouldn't need to worry about setting up a heat lamp. She may scratch against the side for a couple of hours but if she's ready to lay, eventually she will do so. Remember that taking her out of her cage and placing her in this separate container is a last resort and should only be done occasionally.

If you see your female chameleon constantly digging different holes but never see her laying she may be egg bound. If you think this is the case you may need to get help from the vet. Usually this consists of an injection with Oxytocin, which will stimulate her to lay and if this works she will lay her eggs soon after.

Females need a more complex diet compared to males and when they're gravid will need extra attention and misting sessions as well as extra food and supplements. Whilst it may take a lot more time and effort to take care of her, it is still worth considering buying a female because they tend to be naturally tamer, less aggressive and more inclined to interact with humans than males are.

Chapter 4: Vivarium

You should always ensure your housing is set up before you bring home your chameleon. Not only will it make it easier for your new friend to settle in (where would you keep it if you didn't have a vivarium?) but also allows you to get it to the correct temperature and humidity beforehand and therefore hopefully avoiding any health issues. It is important that you have time to play around with the temperatures and humidity so that you can make sure you have the correct levels at all times, especially if this is the first time you've ever owned a chameleon.

Size

As stated previously, Panther chameleons can grow fairly big and therefore need a lot of space. They're arboreal creatures, which means they love to be high up in the trees. The advantage of this is that the cage needs to be taller than it is wide so it doesn't necessarily need to take a lot of room space. A corner would suffice, but remember the bigger the cage, the better.

The recommended minimum size for an adult female is 24 inches (width) x 24 inches (depth) x 36 inches (height) (approximately 61cm x61cm x91 cm).

Males would be the same dimensions but with a height of 48 inches (approximately 122 cm.) However, some owners state that their females are just as active as their males, therefore the taller you can make it the better.

I will point out that a lot of people are buying cages that are classed as 'large' by the retailers but are in fact too short for a Panther chameleon, so take care to ensure that you are buying a cage specifically for this type of creature and not for reptiles in general.

In a pet shop they will usually suggest a smaller cage if you are buying a baby but be aware that a chameleon will grow so fast it will probably only last them until around five or six months if you're lucky. If you can spare the extra expense then there are advantages to having a smaller cage, as it makes eating, drinking and basking less strenuous.

If you don't want to spend money on something that is going to only last a short time then you can put a baby chameleon in an adult cage if they are healthy but as they can easily become lost and may find it difficult to catch food then they will need to be monitored closely. Of course a bigger cage will make monitoring slightly more difficult, as there will be more places to hide.

Whatever you choose to do remember that height needs to be a priority and you should place your cage on a table or cupboard or some other stable surface rather than putting it onto the floor. Remember that your Panther chameleon, although a pet to you, is first and foremost a wild animal and a very territorial one at that. It will most likely view you, your family and any other pets as predators and will feel far more comfortable high up. It should be at least above eye level but as far as your chameleon is concerned the higher you can get them, the better.

Caging Material

The cages you can buy can be made of glass, screen (or mesh) or even wood and there are pros and cons for all of these. The main things to consider when choosing are ventilation, temperature and humidity, so we will look at each one of these in turn.

Ventilation - If your cage isn't properly ventilated then the air will become stale, which can cause respiratory problems. Not only that but stagnant air can also allow fungus and bacteria to grow, again leading to health problems and could potentially result in your chameleon dying.

The good news is screen cages are readily available and less expensive than glass, not only that but they offer good ventilation. When I talk about 'glass' I'm not talking about an aquarium. I hear many people say "oh I have an old fish tank I'm going to put my chameleon in". These are not suitable, as not only are they not tall enough, they don't provide enough ventilation. A glass cage will need a screen or mesh door or ceiling with a fan blowing across the top of the cage, which is placed on the outside not the inside.

Humidity - Whilst a screen cage is excellent for ventilation, it's not so good for humidity. This is where choosing suddenly becomes more difficult, as you need to consider the climate that you live in. If you are in an environment that is humid, a screen cage is probably the perfect choice but if you live in a dry, arid area, glass may be better, as it is easier to manipulate humidity levels if there is less exposure to air outside the cage.

Heat - A wooden or glass cage will retain heat, making it easier to control the temperature but again, both need good ventilation to allow the air to circulate, whereas a screen cage will lose heat. The location of your chameleon's home will be a key factor – is it indoors or outdoors? Do you live in a hot, humid environment or a cold one? For instance, if your chameleon cage is going to be indoors and your home is around 22-24 degrees Celsius (72-75 degrees Fahrenheit) then a screen enclosure with a single lamp could be sufficient enough to provide your chameleon with the temperature range it requires, whereas in the same conditions a glass cage may overheat. In comparison, in cooler climates a screen cage may not be hot enough even with lamps.

Buying a cage therefore isn't as easy as one might think. Glass, wood and mesh are all good options but it is not possible to recommend one over the other without knowing the environment you live in. The best way to choose is to consider the climate your home offers compared to the climate your Panther chameleon requires and decide which enclosure will best meet its needs.

The other option of course is to build your own. The advantage to this is you have the ability to create either a grand masterpiece to be a focal point in the room or a simple, functional habitat in the corner. If you do choose to build your own remember to plan first. The needs of your chameleon should always be top of the list. There's no point making an elaborate cage that looks wonderful if your chameleon can escape or is too cold.

Also consider your budget and skill-set. If you've never built anything in your life this route may not be suitable. A few pieces of wood nailed haphazardly together could end up being more of a danger than a sanctuary for your new pet.

If you do decide on custom-made then be thoughtful and cautious when choosing materials. For instance, glass is expensive and difficult to work with, plastic can melt in high heat, and wood can rot if not treated properly.

Always remember, whichever type of cage you choose, the top must always be a screen. This is because UVB will not penetrate glass or plastic and this is an important requirement for your Panther chameleon.

Make sure it's escape proof and fits snugly on the tank, with strong clips locking it on.

Whichever type of enclosure you choose it is wise to have it set up *before* you bring your chameleon home. Yes, I know I've already said this several times but it is an important rule that potential owners should adhere to. Once it's completed you can keep an eye on humidity, ventilation and temperature before your new pet is exposed to it. This will get you used to checking and adjusting all of these requirements regularly, giving you a better chance of providing a suitable environment that your chameleon will thrive in.

Plants And Branches

Panther chameleons are arboreal creatures, meaning they seek shelter in the uppermost branches and treetops. Lots of leaves to hide amongst will make your new friend feel secure. A lot of people worry that if they put a lot of foliage in the cage the Panther chameleon will hide away and they won't ever see them. I know people who have kept their cages practically bare for this very reason and guess what? Their chameleon had a very short (and unhappy) lifespan. Keeping them in unsuitable conditions is cruel. They are incredibly sensitive creatures and get stressed very easily. First and foremost you are creating a habitat and not an exhibition cage.

This is also a misconception. Yes, your chameleon will hide but once they settle in and feel safe they will start to come out and walk along vines and bask more. If you provide a suitable basking area using branches and a platform underneath the basking light you will be able to see your chameleon whilst it uses this area. You should also have secure perches at different levels and temperatures within the cage. Remember if your chameleon is hiding away so you can't see them, they're doing so for a reason and you need to leave them be.

As well as lots of leaves to hide in, your enclosure will also need lots of sturdy branches, varying in length and diameter for your

39

chameleon to walk across. Their feet are shaped to cling to branches and they dislike walking on flat surfaces. It will also give them exercise. Make sure the plants you use give adequate support. Remember your chameleon should be able to easily navigate their whole enclosure.

You can use fake plants and in some cases these may be preferred as they are easy to clean. However, real plants will help increase and maintain humidity and are better at holding water droplets for drinking, which is important as chameleons don't tend to recognize standing water and therefore won't drink it. As they are also omnivorous and eat vegetable matter, real plants are better if they decide to have a nibble.

The most common ones to use are Pothos, Hibiscus, Umbrella Plants or Ficus Benjamani, Ficus Alii, Ficus Natridia, Dracaenia, Aloe, Spider plants and Philodendrens, which are all reptile safe. Be cautious if you do use Ficus trees, as the sap can be irritating, so this will need to be monitored.

Research each plant you put in beforehand to make sure that you only choose non-toxic ones as well as those that won't die in high humidity. Be careful about bringing in plants and branches from outside, as these can carry parasites that could cause your chameleon to become ill. The plants do not need to be near a window, as they will thrive under the lighting in your chameleon's cage, so don't be tempted to move your chameleon's cage to a window as this can cause them to overheat and will make it more difficult to maintain the correct temperatures.

Substrate
This is simply the material that is used to line the bottom of the cage, also known by some as 'bedding' and is often soil or sand.

This is a controversial topic and one that nobody appears to agree upon. A lot of people will say don't use substrates as it's not necessary. Instead newspaper, paper towels or plastic can be used on the bottom of the cage. The reasons people give for substrate is that it looks a lot nicer and is needed for a female egg laying bin anyway, both of which are true, but if you're a novice and are simply buying it for aesthetic reasons I would discourage you from doing so for the following reasons:

- A substrate can be easily ingested accidentally when the chameleon is catching prey and can get stuck in the digestive tract, causing a blockage that could be potentially fatal. If not fatal it could cost a lot in vet bills!

- Substrate is a breeding ground for bacteria and is harder to clean than newspaper that can just be gathered up and changed.

- Food can hide in the substrate, making it harder to catch, especially for young ones.

To make the vivarium look nicer you could use smooth, black river stones instead. These not only look pretty but also are safer for your chameleon.

Rather than using substrate on the floor of their cage, a lot of people put their plants in pots and put these into the cage. Many people will say that this is suitable because Panther chameleons, tree dwellers by nature, rarely come down from the branches anyway. Whilst this is true you may sometimes see your Panther chameleon on the bottom of your cage, whether it be to find a cooler spot, when hunting prey or, for females, when getting ready to lay their eggs, so I would recommend having some smaller plants or shrubs at the bottom too just in case they do venture down.

If you do decide to use substrate make sure it's one that is non-toxic and easy to clean such as organic, non-fertilized soil and offer food in a clean tub to avoid the risk of ingesting the substrate. Watch your chameleon closely whilst feeding, even if you cup feed, and catch any insects that escape so your chameleon isn't tempted to scurry down to the bottom of the tank after them.

Lighting

This is incredibly important to your chameleons. What may appear to be nothing more than a simple light bulb to you is actually a necessity that your Panther chameleon is physically dependent upon. Bodily functions such as thermoregulation, calcium absorption and even the ability to see will require a spectrum of lighting. How much in depth knowledge you have about these lights is crucial to your success as a chameleon owner.

UVB Bulbs – These are critical. Ultraviolet-B – or UVB – is present in sunlight and the majority of animals on Earth will have some level of exposure to it, but reptiles have a particular need for UVB. We humans absorb UVB and if someone has low Vitamin D levels a doctor will often recommend they sit out in the sun. Panther chameleons are no different. They absorb Vitamin D from the sunlight and convert this to Vitamin D3. No D3 means calcium cannot be utilized in their system. This can lead to the chameleon gradually developing physical problems such as stunted growth, soft eggs (in females) and recent studies have also linked lack of UVB to poor immune system. A leading killer in the reptile industry is Metabolic Bone Disease (MBD) where the chameleon's bones slowly deteriorate, eventually becoming brittle and malformed. It's incredibly painful yet can be easily avoided by fitting a UVB light bulb.

A common mistake people make is they go off and buy the strongest UVB bulb they can find, after all these creatures live out in the desert and are constantly in the sunlight out in the wild, right? However, too much UVB can be harmful and over exposure can shorten their lifespan. Like everything else when it comes to chameleons, the right balance is the key. Medium levels should be sufficient for most types of cages, so make sure to check it is suitable before purchasing.

UVA Bulbs- Whilst this doesn't contribute to the lifespan of the chameleon it does affect their ability to see, so I believe it is in the creature's best interest to include it here.

It is thought that reptiles can detect a larger spectrum of lighting than us mere humans can, so although UVA is invisible to us, without it your chameleon's vision can be impaired. Some scientists have compared it to color blindness whilst some say not providing it is akin to forcing the chameleon to live its life in a darkened room and it is thought that it affects appetite and reproduction. Some studies have shown that females will seek out UV light when preparing to lay eggs. The importance of UVA light is still under investigation and many people are skeptical but others believe owners are neglecting the psychological well being of these animals by not including it.

I'll let you make your own mind up but my point of view is if you want to create a perfect environment for your chameleon rather than just an okay, suitable for a couple of years cage then everything needs to be considered, even invisible (to us) light. After all, what is the cost of a light bulb or two compared to limited vision for your beloved pet?

Basking Lights - Thermoregulation is the term used in reference to a cold-blooded animals' ability to control its body temperature by moving from warmer to cooler spots. Your Panther chameleon thermo-regulates manually by moving from shade to sunlight as their body temperature changes. For a complete setup a chameleon requires a basking light, which should be a hot surface in a corner near the top, and will be their main source of heat.

Night - Being diurnal (meaning they sleep at night and are awake in the daytime)**,** Panther chameleons must have distinct day and night periods, just like in the wild, to maintain their biological rhythms. All lights should be switched off to allow for around 12 hours of darkness with a slight drop in temperature. It is okay for daylight hours to change seasonally as they would if your Panther chameleon was outside, so their inside habitat should reflect the same. However, daylight periods must be light and nighttime periods must be dark. The best way to ensure all the lights get switched off is to have them on a timer. Your Panther chameleon's cage needs to be in a room away from any noise and light from the rest of the household so they get a sufficient amount of sleep.

Full Spectrum Bulbs - If you go into a pet shop you will see Full Spectrum Bulbs and will probably be told they're the best thing for your chameleon, after all it says right there on the packaging that it provides every form of light a reptile will ever need – heat, UVB, UVA and so on.

Again, these are controversial amongst chameleon owners because most compact bulbs are incapable of providing a significant amount of UVB output, so choose wisely and research which best suits your enclosure before purchasing.

A UV tube may be a better option and a T5 tube is recommended, as if it's attached to the ceiling with a reflector it can send UVB rays to approximately 60 centimeters (24 inches) and will last around nine months before needing to be replaced. T8 units are also available but these only travel approximately 30 centimeters (12 inches) and will only last roughly six months.

Remembering to replace your UVB lights is important so make a note of when you buy them, otherwise it can be difficult to tell because although they may still switch on they may not be sending out high enough levels of UVB. They're definitely worth investing in, after all a UVB light replacement could end up being a lot cheaper than the vet fees that could result from a sick, unhappy chameleon.

All lights should be on top of the cage on the outside shining downwards. As chameleons have a tendency to climb anything they can, keeping lights on the inside poses a risk of burns.

Gradient Temperature
For them to thermo-regulate, it is essential that you provide your chameleon with a gradient of temperatures within their habitat to allow them to do this. This means it needs to be cooler on the bottom and warmer at the top so the chameleon can move in and out of the heat as it needs to. This is also why you need to provide plenty of plants for shade, as the Panther chameleon needs to have the means to cool itself down to prevent overheating. The temperature of the cage needs to be monitored daily using a thermometer with a probe or an infrared temperature gun if possible. You can buy stick on ones fairly cheap but these are highly inaccurate. Make sure you check the temperature in different places to ensure that there are plenty of cool spots and plenty of hot spots.

It is important to make sure you adjust the temperature if necessary, otherwise your chameleon can become sick with respiratory disease. They may also stop eating, as without proper heat and light they have trouble digesting.

If you keep your Panther chameleon inside then as long as your house doesn't drop to 17 degrees Celsius or below (approximately

63 degrees Fahrenheit) it shouldn't be necessary to heat your cage at night.

A guide to temperature:

Daytime: Ambient temperature 24-27 degrees Celsius (75-80 degrees Fahrenheit).

Basking Spot: 32 - 35degrees Celsius (90-95 degrees Fahrenheit).

Night: above 17 degrees Celsius (63 degrees Fahrenheit).

Some sources say that Panther chameleons can temporarily tolerate temperature changes but it is not recommended that you fluctuate from the above too much. The drop at nighttime is necessary because it slows down their metabolism and facilitates heavy sleeping. Chameleons will not rest well at night if it's too hot.

In the morning your Panther chameleon will head straight up to the basking spot, which is important as this speeds up their metabolism, allowing them to hunt and digest their food properly.

Baby chameleons should be kept a bit cooler than adults during the day so an ambient temperature of 22-26 degrees Celsius (72-80 degrees Fahrenheit) and a basking spot of around 28 degrees Celsius (82 degrees Fahrenheit) should be sufficient for one that is nine months or younger. This is because younger animals aren't always good at thermoregulation and may not get out of the heat when they need to. Instead they tend to open their mouths to cool themselves down rather than moving to a different spot. If you see this with your chameleon, whatever the age, it is worth checking the temperatures and adjusting if necessary.

Habitat Maintenance

Every day you should spot clean your Panther chameleon's cage removing any feces, shed skin, soiled substrate (if you're using some) and uneaten food – basically anything that can go moldy, grow bacteria or start to smell.

Their fecal matter can carry salmonella, which can be passed onto humans, so be sure to thoroughly wash your hands immediately after coming into contact with your chameleon or their cage.

At least once a month you should remove everything and thoroughly clean the entire tank using a mild disinfectant. These can be bought but you should always check that they are suitable for your chameleon – I always check online to see what other owners/breeders are using –just remember to follow the instructions properly. You can use a mild dishwashing liquid as long as it is diluted in warm water and then use either a vinegar and water mixture (one part vinegar to eight parts water) or a very, very weak bleach and water solution (one part bleach to thirty two parts water) and wash everything down again with this. Please make sure you just use one or the other – DO NOT use bleach and vinegar together as it makes a solution that is toxic to chameleons.

Whatever you use always make sure it is a weak concentration. Wash down the cage and any 'furniture' such as the plants and stones then rinse everything off thoroughly with plain water. If you do use substrate such as sand then you should use a sieve to clean out any other bits of debris that may have got caught up in it. Once everything is clean and rinsed off put everything back in. If you can keep it as identical as possible your chameleon will be a lot happier and less stressed, as they won't have to get used to new surroundings every time you clean.

When you do the daily spot clean it is fine for your chameleon to stay in the cage and an advantage to this is they will get used to you opening and closing their cage door, however when you do the deep clean your chameleon should be put in a temporary cage, out of the way of the detergents and should only be put back in when everything is thoroughly rinsed and dried off.

Chapter 5: Watering And Drainage

A common health problem with captive Panther chameleons is dehydration. Every living creature needs water but unlike pets such as cats or dogs, keeping a Panther chameleon hydrated isn't as easy as putting down a bowl of water and changing it every day. Again, successfully hydrating your chameleon means understanding how they live in the wild and trying to mimic these conditions as closely as possible.

Chameleons don't recognize standing water so out in the wild a Panther chameleon will get water by licking morning dew from the leaves, soaking themselves in rainfalls and, during dry periods, eating leaves. A dirty puddle of water pooled on the floor will not entice them to drink so you need to ensure you have a good watering system in place.

Misting
The best way to simulate the natural drinking habit of a chameleon in the wild is by misting. This simply means spraying a fine mist over their cage every few hours during daylight hours only, ensuring all your leaves and even the chameleon itself gets a good soaking, as this will help keep them moist, making shedding easier. This misting is meant to mimic rain and the chameleon will then sip water droplets from the leaves. Remember some chameleons are shyer than others and you may have one that won't eat or drink in front of you, which is why real plants are sometimes better than fake ones, as they tend to hold the water better and if your chameleon is particularly thirsty they may start to nibble a few in order to get extra water.

The first misting session should be around one hour after you switch the lights on. Keep in mind the first thing your chameleon will do upon waking is head on up to their basking spot to raise their temperature. The last thing they want at this time is to be drenched in water, as this can lower their body temperature. It's akin to someone throwing a bucket of water over you or dragging you under a cold shower as soon as your eyes open – not a pleasant experience.

You should also allow around three or four hours between misting and the final misting should be done at least two hours before you switch the lights off for the night to ensure the enclosure has time to dry out. You don't want a soggy, waterlogged environment for your chameleon. Again, you're imitating an environment that is humid and where dew and rain dries out pretty quickly.

One way of misting is with a spray bottle, which are cheap and can be bought for around £1-£5 ($1-$5 in the US). You may even already have one lying around at home but just make sure that if you do use one you find in the cupboard that it isn't one that has ever had any chemicals in. Chameleons are so sensitive anyway that using a bottle that had chemicals in, even if it has been thoroughly washed out, can cause problems.

You can also mist with a pressurized spray bottle. These are slightly more expensive but tend to create a finer mist than regular spray bottles. Your chameleon may prefer being sprinkled with a light, small mist rather than the hard drenching it may get from a cheaper bottle. Most hardware or garden stores should have these pressurized water pumps and they cost anything from £10 upwards (prices start from $13 upwards in the US). Of course you can buy proper ones specially made for chameleons and reptiles in pet shops or online these will cost you around £59.99 upwards (prices in the US start from around $63 upwards), but again you may prefer to have something more specialized so that you can be safe in the knowledge that you are using something suitable.

Before you decide to cut costs and buy a cheap misting bottle consider how practical it is for you to hand mist. If you are indoors all day or you can be flexible in the times you go out then it may be okay for you to do this, but if you work it becomes more difficult. For instance, say you leave the house at 8 am, you will need to mist before you go. If you decide to do this at 7.30am then you need to switch the lights on at 6.30am to give your chameleon an hour to bask. The next misting will need to be around 10.30am and again around 1.30pm. You can then get the last one in around 4.30pm, giving the enclosure two hours to dry before you turn the lights out at 6.30pm so the Panther chameleon can get its required twelve hours of darkness. Each misting session should be anything from two – five minutes. If you are home all day or your commute from work is fairly quick so you can come back at lunch time then you can probably do it but if you are out of the house for eight hours or more at a time then you may need to invest in an automatic misting system, again these are more expensive but are reliable and convenient and could be worth the time it saves in the long run.

You may read that it is acceptable to mist for five minutes twice a day and although this could be enough to keep your chameleon alive, if you want to keep a healthy chameleon in as perfect an environment as possible so they lead a long and happy life then you need to mist more often. It is worth noting that there is a lot of contradictory information regarding the length of time you should mist and how often. This is because everyone's environment is different so it is all-dependent upon the temperatures in your house as well as their enclosure. If you mist and it hasn't dried up within two hours then you may have to use shorter misting sessions. If you find the water has all gone within half an hour or so you may need a longer session, as your chameleon may not have chance to drink the water otherwise.

You could use an automatic misting system, which will set you back around £52.99 upwards in the UK. (In the US prices start from around $56).

Water needs to be clean and free from chlorine and heavy metals. If you use tap water you will need to treat it first, a better choice therefore would be bottled or natural spring water. Do not use distilled water, as this lacks the minerals your chameleon needs.

Again this is another topic that people disagree on and I think this is dependent once more on the area you live in and the quality of water you have. Some say distilled should only be used because of course in the wild chameleons only drink rainwater and to not use distilled will provide too many minerals. I think if you are raising a chameleon that has been captive bred then you should ask the breeder what they have been using, but it would just be a case of adjusting supplementation to balance out the extra minerals they are getting in the water.

Whatever you use should be around room temperature at minimum, the warmer the better. It should cool down as it sprays out but you should always check the temperature beforehand. Panther chameleons don't like cold water so please don't use it. Be careful not to soak baby chameleons, as their little nostrils can become clogged up, causing them to aspirate. Instead just spray the leaves of the plants around them. For babies I find it's better to mist for less time, more often.

Drippers
A dripper system provides a constant supply of fresh water into the cage throughout the day so your chameleon won't go thirsty between misting sessions. It usually consists of a round tub with a closable top and a nozzle to adjust the drip speed as well as a tube, which directs water where it is needed and sits on top of the creature's enclosure. It is a handy product and can be bought for around £10 in the UK (around $13 in the US) depending on the size you want.

Some people don't buy drippers and opt instead to make their own by poking a small hole in the bottom of a container such as a plastic cup or peanut butter jar and hang this at the top of the enclosure.

Underneath they have another container to catch the drips so that their cages don't become water logged. These containers need to be covered with a mesh sheet so that your chameleon cannot climb in and nor can any live insects you feed your chameleon – crickets for instance are attracted to water. If you did decide to try and make your own be sure that the water drips slowly and at a fairly regular rate rather than gushing out all at once and put it somewhere safe, out of reach of your chameleon and make sure it is secure enough that it won't fall. Remember the effect you're going for is that of dew drops on leaves not a downpour or a swimming pool.

Waterfalls And Taps

This is another controversial topic but I include it in here because a lot of people think that as a chameleon doesn't recognize standing water then a waterfall is a good solution. Look online and for every person saying "yes they look lovely and my Panther chameleon loves drinking from it" you will find at least another three more shouting "no, don't do it, they're death traps!"

The reason they're so controversial is that a chameleon probably won't drink from a waterfall and so they are deemed pointless by owners. Instead these creatures tend to defecate in them, making them a breeding ground for bacteria, which can in turn make your pet sick. Live crickets and other insects can also get caught in them and drown, which could mean your chameleon gets less food than it ought to be having and they just end up looking messy.

My opinion is don't bother but if you do decide to buy one then make sure it's kept clean and the water is draining well. I don't think it is a substitute for misting and dripping and I would always recommend these methods for providing your chameleon with water over a waterfall.

And taps? I have seen lots of pictures that people have posted online of their Panther chameleon drinking from a running tap. I hate these photographs. Yes, their chameleon may be happy but my gut instinct is that they aren't. I don't recommend this either. Although they are a pet to you, they are wild creatures and aren't going to be drinking from taps in the rainforest therefore I would always stick to misting and drippers.

Drainage
With all this water it will only be a matter of time before your cage starts to resemble a swamp and/or overflow. Some people simply use towels at the bottom of the cage along with a container placed underneath the dripper but really proper drainage is better suited if you want to create an optimum enclosure as close to the wild environment as possible.

If the bottom of your cage is solid you will need to drill a hole in it (need I say before your chameleon is living there?). There are many creative ways to create drainage systems for indoor cages so it is worth looking online for ideas. Remember your cage needs to be high up, so a lot of people opt for drilling holes into the bottom of the cage and then placing it on a metal shelving unit (the kind with the bars in rather than a solid shelf) with a plastic container such as a bin directly underneath.

One person I know had a cheap chest of drawers and they drilled holes into the bottom of the cage and the top of the chest of drawers. The water drained from the cage into the top drawer, which meant they just had to pull this out to empty it.

When drilling holes be strategic and look at where the water will naturally end up so you can place the holes in the correct place. There's no point having two drainage holes on the right hand side if the water is pooling into the middle.

Just remember, whatever sort of system you use, empty whatever container you have in place to catch water so that it doesn't overflow. The last thing you want in your lounge (or whatever room you are using) is a bin full of dirty, stagnant, smelly water.
One more thing to note is if you have holes in the bottom of your cage and you put live feeders in for your chameleon to hunt there is a risk that these insects will escape, so it might be an idea to cover the bottom of the cage with a sheet of thin plastic or something similar at meal times.

Please don't ignore the importance of drainage and leave puddles of water on your cage floor. Not only will it make a mess, but it will soon become dirty and lead to health issues.

Chapter 6: Feeding

Gut Loading

This means feeding the insects you are going to be giving to your Panther chameleon a healthy and nutritious diet of fresh fruit and vegetables about twenty-four hours before giving them to your chameleon, as these nutrients will then be passed on. For example, if you want your chameleon to get enough Vitamin A you can do this by feeding leafy green vegetables to the crickets before putting them in the cage. Although I will talk about supplements further down, most reptile veterinarians agree that gut loading is the best way to provide your chameleon the nutrients it needs, after all, in the wild the insects are not 'dusted' with vitamins and the more you can duplicate their natural habitat and habits the healthier and happier it will be.

Crickets, cockroaches and mealworms are easy to gut-load and should be included in your feeding plan. Crickets in particular will devour fruits and vegetables so they make an ideal food source. To gut-load simply put the insects in a tub with fresh vegetables or fruits and leave them for twenty-four hours. Of course be careful that they have a lid on so they can't escape but this needs to be mesh or have holes so the crickets still get air, otherwise they will die.

Feeders

Your Panther chameleon needs protein, so the majority of their diet should be comprised of insects. Again, think about how these highly specialized creatures hunt in the wild. High in the treetops of subtropical or tropical forests, they are eating a wide variety of insects, both from the air and the trees all around them. You can never hope to duplicate these conditions exactly, it's impossible. For one thing, the insects that you could catch are dependent upon where you live and where would you keep them all or find the time to hunt them every day? However you should aim to get as close as possible by feeding your chameleon a variety. They will get a much more nutritional diet if you're offering four or five different insects rather than just a 'cricket only' diet, no matter how much you gut-load them first. Below is a list of the insects that these chameleons can eat in captivity.

Crickets – These are a staple of chameleon feeding because they are easy to obtain and easy to gut-load because they will eat pretty much anything. Feed the crickets fresh greens and slices of sweet potato or carrot to give them nutrition. Also provide them with a water source that won't allow them to drown such as a piece of juicy fruit or a wet sponge. Gut-loaded crickets can comprise up to 80% of your chameleon's total diet but they do have a low calcium/phosphorus ratio so additional calcium supplementation should be included with most cricket meals. Supplement lightly with pure calcium powder, not one with vitamins.

You will need to feed baby and juvenile chameleons smaller crickets. Black crickets tend to bite chameleons at night, so brown crickets are safer.

Please do not feed your crickets dog food. By doing this not only are you missing an opportunity to add nutritional value, but also some dog foods contain artificial additives that can be harmful to your chameleon.

Locusts – These are often a great staple food because they are nutritious, have good longevity and are easy to keep. A small water source, some basic food and a plastic container at room temperature is all that is needed to keep these insects active and healthy for a number of weeks. Locusts are active and have vibrant colors, making them great at arousing a resting chameleon's interest and tempting it away from its basking spot.

Silkworms – This is the larva of the Silk Moth. They are good because they have a high nutritional value and can be used without dusting. You can also let them develop into moths and feed these to your chameleon too.

Mealworms – These are beetle larvae and many pet stores sell them in small plastic tubs. Like crickets, they can be gut-loaded to increase nutritional value. However, remember to store these in the refrigerator because otherwise they will pupate and turn into beetles. "Giant mealworms" can bite so you will need to be careful how you handle them.

A lot of people will tell you to squish their heads before feeding, otherwise the worm can bite your chameleon's mouth or stomach but most chameleons chew these thoroughly before eating so this shouldn't be a problem. They do have a high fat content so should only really be given as a treat, otherwise it can be harmful to your chameleon's health. The hard chitin shell of the mealworm is not digestible and can cause blockage of the gut.

Waxworms (Sometimes called Grubs) – These are a type of moth larvae and can be purchased at pet stores, as they are a feeder insect for a wide variety of reptiles as well as fish and birds. They are plump and waxy (hence the name), full of moisture and easy to store, however they are not as nutritious as the other items on this list and, like mealworms, have a high fat content so they shouldn't make up the chameleon's main diet. Instead they should be given now and again as a treat and to add variety to their diet. Lightly dust before feeding to increase their nutritional value.

Be aware that some chameleons love them so much they become addicted and will refuse to eat anything else. The best way to avoid this is to feed only in moderation. They are a great insect to use when hand feeding. Try to feed them when they are white in color, as this means they have shed their hard shell, which can cause blockages. You can also feed them to your chameleon when they have turned into moths.

Butterworms – These are the larvae of the Chilean Moth. They are a contrast of red and yellow in color and apparently have a sweet, buttery scent. They have high levels of calcium, which make them a great treat. However you can't gut-load them because in the wild they only eat one type of leaf, which is that of the Tebo tree. Instead you need to put them in your refrigerator, which will slow their metabolism and keep them in a hibernated state. They should also be used with caution, as they have been known to cause a reaction in chameleons and whilst there is no scientific evidence to support this there are a number of cases with the same symptoms being reported and linked to these insects.

Hornworms –There are two kinds of hornworms a chameleon can eat – Tomato Hornworms and Tobacco Hornworms, named after the plants they feed on. You have them shipped to you live in little containers then feed them until they grow into large worms. If you let them pupate they will turn into Hawk Moths. If you don't mind having moths flying around you could let one or two pupate and feed them to your chameleon in moth form; they may chase it down and devour it. I've included them here because if you do an Internet search for what to feed a chameleon then these are high on the list, however be aware that if you're in the UK/Europe they are actually banned so pet stores won't stock them. This is because they can survive and breed here, becoming a threat to the tomato industry.

Grasshoppers – These are found within the natural range of most chameleon species but you may have a harder time finding them. You don't have to feed them to your chameleon but as they are larger and 'meatier' than crickets they will provide a lot of nourishment. These need to be kept in a dry environment and be fed fresh greens or grass to get moisture.

Superworms or Zoophobias- Superworms look like mealworms but are far bigger and have slightly different coloring. Like crickets and mealworms they need to be fed a diet of fresh fruits and vegetables before giving them to your chameleon. What makes them better than mealworms is that there is more body than hard shell. Again you want to wait until they have just shed their hard shell and are white in color. They are not suitable for baby or juvenile chameleons and should only be fed when your lizard is big enough to eat them.

Flies – These are included because in the wild chameleons will eat them but they don't offer as much nutrition as the insects mentioned above and as you would have to buy them from maggots, feed them until they pupate and then put them into the cage (at the risk of having them escape and buzz around your house or else remove the wings first) they are often more trouble than they're worth so many keepers skip them altogether. Flightless fruit flies however are a great food for your baby chameleon and can be bought ready to eat.

You should always try to have at least three different feeders on hand and rotate them to stop your chameleon getting bored, as they can go on a hunger strike for long periods when subjected to the same diet over and over.

Wild-caught insects should not be used unless you are absolutely sure they have not been exposed to pesticides, insecticides, parasites or metal poisoning. If you do decide to use wild caught then locusts, grasshoppers, katydids and dragonflies are all good options. You can also use certain moths but you need to research about their toxicity first.

A good rule when feeding is to always give proper-sized prey that is suitable for the size of your chameleon. Prey should never be longer than the width of their head. This means smaller crickets will be needed for babies.

If you are feeding larger insects make sure they're soft bodied or have shed first, as an insect with a large exoskeleton is often difficult to digest and may cause impaction.

Leaves

Panther chameleons aren't strict carnivores but rather are omnivorous creatures, meaning they will eat plants as well as insects. This is thought to be because they live in dry, arid conditions, eating plants is a way of obtaining water. Therefore, whilst vegetation isn't necessarily important for their diet, you may find that the plants in their habitat gradually start to disappear. This isn't true for all and some captive bred chameleons won't eat vegetation at all but if you do want to offer it from time to time then try a few leaves of kale, rocket or spring greens chopped up, watercress, carrot or sweet potato (the latter should be both grated and chopped small). Other vegetation can be offered but chameleons seem to prefer soft leaves.

Dandelion leaves are a good replacement for spring greens and watercress but if you pick them from outside make sure you choose areas that are free from pesticides.

I always think it's a great idea to wash any vegetable matter in warm water first before giving it to your chameleon, especially any that you've found outside. Not only does this ensure that they are free from harmful bacteria, insects or dirt that could become compacted in their gut, all of which can make them ill, but also because if they are slightly wet it may make them more tempting for your chameleon and gives them that extra drinking water. Try different leaves and vegetables to see which your chameleon prefers.

Supplements

Even when gut-loading, a lot of experts recommend that feeder insects are dusted with a good quality calcium supplement fortified with Vitamin D3 before being fed. Avoid those supplements with added phosphorous unless specifically directed to by the vet, as too much of this can cause kidney disease. Juveniles should have their food dusted daily, whilst adults can be reduced to 2-3 times a week. Pregnant or gravid females should also have their food dusted more often, as they will need additional calcium supplements during this time.

Dusting means exactly that – a very light dusting. Don't smother your feeder insects in supplements, as if your chameleon gets too high a dose this can be dangerous to their health.

It is difficult to say exactly how much your chameleon should be supplemented because each one is different depending on their owner and set up. If your Panther chameleon is going outside and getting a high level of natural sunlight and you are gut-loading your crickets and other insects thoroughly then they may need less Vitamin D3 and Calcium than one that never goes outside.
It is important that you don't over supplement, so although you can use this as a guide it is always recommended that you talk to a vet.

How To Feed

There are a variety of different ways to feed your Panther chameleon. Some people will simply let the crickets or feeders loose in the cage for the chameleon to hunt (known as free ranging). This gives them exercise and recreates more of a natural situation that they would encounter in the wild. However, some chameleons will not hunt for food or eat whilst somebody is watching them and crickets and other small creatures can easily escape unless you have cricket proofed your cage thoroughly. A smaller chameleon in a large cage may also struggle to hunt and find all of the prey you have let loose in the cage.

Another way to feed live insects is to put them in a plastic cup and securely hang them or attaching them to a tree or branch inside the cage using twist ties. If you place some small pieces of fruit or vegetables into the cup as well then your feeder insects will continue to gut-load whilst they're waiting to be eaten. This means your Panther chameleon will still get the nutrients even if they don't actually eat the fruit or vegetables themselves.

Make sure the cup is clean each time you feed and if you have more than one chameleon make sure you use different containers to feed each one to avoid potential cross contamination of bacteria or disease.

Keep the feeding cup low in the tree or on a branch near the bottom of the cage. This is because chameleons like to hunt their prey and will usually approach from an upward position as this helps them to avoid the top or side of the feeding container. Most chameleons can be easily trained to feed from a cup and may even come to expect food to be in there.

Some people will hand feed if their chameleon will let them and whilst this is good for bonding it shouldn't be done for every meal. You can also use tweezers or small tongs if you don't want to touch the insects.

When Should You Feed And How Often?
You should feed your Panther chameleon in the morning, not long after their lights are turned on if possible. Feeding in the evenings or at nighttime, although more convenient for you to watch them, isn't

recommended because it can be unhealthy to your Panther chameleon, as they need the heat and activity during daylight hours in order to digest their food.

Babies should be given a constant supply of food, ideally in small amounts but as often as possible; the general rule is you feed as much as they can eat.

Juvenile chameleons should be fed around 10-15 crickets daily. You need to be very careful not to overfeed and this life stage is the most difficult for a lot of chameleon owners. There is a high risk of developing Metabolic Bone Disease by overfeeding or misjudging the calcium to food ratio. Instead of offering a high volume of food, which can make it difficult to manage supplementation, offer food little and often so your chameleon can grow steadily and slowly. At this stage you can also introduce worms such as silkworms.

An adult Panther chameleon (18 months and above) should be fed around 6-8 full-sized crickets a day. At this stage they can also be offered treats. Your Panther chameleon may be wary of new foods at first as they may not recognize it as food, but once they've taken a few bites you may find that they go crazy for whatever insect you've introduced.

Although you may not want to reduce the amount of food your adult chameleon eats, it is important to cut down on their daily intake once they stop growing. Panther chameleons in captivity aren't as active as they would be in the wild because they have limited space. Also remember that in the wild they may not find food every day whereas in captivity they are being fed the same amount at the same time each day, which can lead to them becoming overweight. Ideally you want your chameleon to be lean rather than too fat or too skinny in order to be healthy.

I've only put the food amounts in crickets here, as for most people this will be the main staple food that they feed the majority of the time. If you are providing a variety then just substitute this for crickets. For instance if you are feeding your adult Panther chameleon a couple of mealworms one day then provide them with a couple less crickets.

What To Avoid

There are lots of insects that are poisonous to chameleons. These include ladybirds, fireflies, spiders (certain ones are poisonous but the best way is to avoid them all unless you are absolutely sure they're okay), scorpions, centipedes, hairy caterpillars and other poisonous insects as well as bees, wasps and anything that stings – always check before you feed anything new to your chameleon. The list of what to feed and what to avoid is too vast to include everything here.

You can buy canned crickets but these don't have high nutritional value. Just like with human food, fresh is best.

A question many people will ask is "can I feed dead insects to my chameleon?" Live insects are preferable because moving insects will catch their attention whereas dead insects won't. If you have live insects that you are gut-loading which suddenly die you shouldn't really feed these either unless you are certain of what caused their death, as they may have eaten something or be host to some sort of parasite that could make your chameleon ill.

If the food that is uneaten isn't captured then they can turn on your chameleon and start to bite them so make sure you clear the cage afterwards.

Chapter 7: Settling In

As tempting as it may be, don't buy your Panther chameleon on a whim. Don't ever say "I'm just going to look" if you know you have no willpower to say "no thank you, I'm just looking today".

To be a responsible chameleon owner you need to have its new home set up in advance. You need to have had at least a few days checking the temperature and humidity levels and adjusting wherever necessary to ensure that these are correct for when your chameleon moves in. Only when this set up is prepared and correct can you buy your chameleon.

If you buy your chameleon from the Internet or mail order it will most likely arrive in a small box. Travelling will have been a frightening ordeal and the creature will need time to adjust to its new surroundings. If the box they arrive in is small enough to put in their cage, do so and let your chameleon venture out when it's ready.

Although you will probably be dying to pick them up straight away or spend hours staring at them, resist the temptation and put their well being first. These creatures don't like feeling as if they're being watched, so if possible cover their cage with a thin blanket and leave them alone to get used to their new surroundings. It is important to make sure everyone else in the household does the same, including children. Keep any other pets away too and make sure the room they're in is kept as quiet as possible. Other than feeding and spot cleaning the cage, you should ignore your new chameleon altogether. As I said in the beginning, this may seem cruel, but they aren't friendly animals like puppies; they need time to adjust and relax.

This should be the same process for any chameleon of any age, no matter where you bought it. Remember if it came from a pet shop or a previous owner (even if you've bought it from a private seller with its cage and everything in it), its outside surroundings have still changed. It's still had to travel to get to you and it's now got to get used to new sights and smells.

After a couple of days you should be able to remove the cover, although it's important that you continue to use this at night in order for your chameleon to get a good night's sleep.

During the acclimating process avoid rearranging, adding or removing any plants, rocks or 'furniture' in the cage. The territory is unfamiliar enough and any changes, no matter how small, will make it more difficult for your chameleon to settle.

A good way to get your new pet familiar with its new home is to put some live crickets loose in their cage. This will give them an activity as well as encouraging movement, which in turn helps them map out the layout of their cage. Use small (nymphs not adults) crickets that have been dusted and release them on the sidewalls or vines. Keep them climbing, as if they fall on the floor they will most likely die and won't garner much interest.

Don't worry if your new chameleon doesn't eat for a few days when you first buy it. It is a normal reaction to a new environment. It will be assessing for threats and predators, and once it feels settle then it will start to eat. If you feed them live crickets and cover the cage they may feel more comfortable to hunt knowing nobody is watching them.

New chameleons that are afraid to expose themselves may opt to hide in the middle or back of the cage throughout the day and may even avoid basking. Although this is normal, it means their body temperature may not increase enough to enable good digestion, which will in turn have an effect on eating. If this is a concern you have then, if possible, raise the overall room temperature to around 27-28 degrees Celsius (mid 70s Fahrenheit). As your chameleon starts to feel secure they will begin to bask by themselves and you can adjust the room temperature again accordingly.

Once your chameleon stays in open view once the cover is removed, they are starting to settle. If they continue to stay out whenever you're near the cage rather than trying to hide as soon as you cast a shadow over their enclosure then you're already a third of the way to taming (see next chapter).

Chapter 8: Handling And Free Ranging

A lot of chameleon owners have stated that they can handle their Panther chameleons without causing stress and indeed there are a number of videos and photographs that have been posted on the Internet of seemingly calm Panther chameleons interacting with their owners, whether that be eating out of their hand, sitting on their heads or shoulders or being held gently on their lap being stroked.

This is being held as proof that these types of chameleons can be tamed. Whilst I'm not condemning people who do this as bad owners, I would remind you here that chameleons are wild animals and there is far more evidence to suggest that they don't enjoy being handled than there is to the contrary, so handling is not recommended.

These animals are sensitive and my view is that they should be treated like exotic fish – observed but not to touch. I don't believe these creatures ever truly 'bond' with their owners, despite what some people say. There are those that state their chameleons come straight over and climb on their hand as soon as they open the cage door because they have a strong bond. Although I can't possibly say for certain how every chameleon in captivity feels the negative part of me thinks that these chameleons simply associate their owner with food and know that this is a way of getting insects.

What these anecdotes do show, together with the aforementioned photographs on the Internet, is that it is possible in some cases to pick them up without causing too much undue harm or distress.

Time
This will take a lot of work and time. You're not going to wake up one morning to find your chameleon running over to the door of its enclosure excited to see you. Nor is your baby chameleon going to

jump out of its box and give you a great big hug as soon as you've purchased it. Instead it is a gradual bonding and understanding that will only come over time as your chameleon starts to see you as less of a threat.

It is suggested that you spend at least fifteen minutes a day to work on bonding. Try and choose the same time every day to develop a routine so your chameleon will know when to expect you.

Timing is also key - only try to handle your chameleon if it is near the front of its cage, either climbing on the door or ceiling or if it's sat on a branch near the front. If your chameleon is hiding in the back or center of the cage or is under its basking light then leave it alone. I cannot stress this enough. Reaching deep inside a chameleon's cage is along the same lines as trespassing and will only hinder your attempts to bond by stressing your chameleon out more and making it feel unsafe and insecure.

Temperament
Although it is thought that Panther chameleons are one of the 'friendlier' breeds (if a chameleon can indeed be termed friendly), whether yours reacts well to handling will depend on their temperament. Just like people, some are friendlier and more docile whilst others are grumpy and aggressive. You may simply end up with one who is in the latter group and will hate any contact despite how patient you are and how much time you invest in them.

Unfortunately this is simply bad luck, but I urge you to enjoy your chameleon from afar and love them anyway. Even if you never touch them, they are such fascinating creatures to watch and for a true chameleon lover just being able to observe them will bring endless joy. Please don't buy a Panther chameleon with the sole purpose of being able to handle them and show them off on the Internet and to your friends.

A baby chameleon will get used to handling better than a juvenile, although that isn't to say an older chameleon won't ever let you handle them, just that it may take a lot longer to establish that initial bond. How the chameleon has been treated by humans in the past will also affect their mood. For instance, small-scale breeders will often handle and pamper their babies from the day they hatch so these chameleons will become used to handling. This is because most breeders know a lot of owners will want to be able to pick them up at some point and it is handy if ever you need to take them out of their cage to clean it, take them outside for natural sunlight or to take them to the vets for a medical check-up. However, wherever you buy a chameleon from you need to be aware that if it has been mistreated then naturally the chameleon it will be wary.

Their journey to you will also have an effect on their personality. Most chameleons are put in dark boxes when travelling to or from pet shops or - if you purchased from the Internet – to get to you. If your chameleon's journey was traumatic it will take a long time for it to get used to its new surroundings and feel settled, so you should always take this into account before even thinking about handling.

How To Handle
The best way to start is with food in order to garner their interest and gain their trust. If you have been cup feeding then the best way to do this is to hold the cup during feeding instead of hanging it on a tree. Your chameleon may back away or display signs of aggression the first few times you do this and if you see these signs you should always secure the cup in its usual place, shut the cage and leave them alone. You can keep trying each day until your chameleon eventually settles. This may take weeks, months or longer but if you persevere eventually you should notice a change. Just remember to always back off immediately at the first sign of stress.

Once they seem fine with you holding the cup for them then the next stage is hand feeding. If you are trying to handle your chameleon then you should have had them long enough to know which snacks they enjoy. Place one of these either in the palm of your hand or between your fingers. The palm is often better because chameleons often mistake fingers as food. Open the cage very slowly - another thing I can't emphasize enough. Whenever you handle your chameleon or are near its cage, your movements need to be incredibly slow so as not to spook them.

Watch your chameleon very carefully. If they don't retreat then hold the prey around 20 cm (8 inches) from them – remember their tongue is very long! Their eyes should be fixed on the prey not on you. If your chameleon sees the prey but then is more focused on you – think of that frightened, 'rabbit caught in headlights' type look – give up and try again later. Remember the objective here is to gain your chameleon's trust; it's a long-term relationship you want to build not a temporary, forced one.

Make brief eye contact when you first open the cage but then turn your head away slightly so you can still see what they're doing but you're not staring. Never stare, as this can be seen as threatening. No matter how much you love them, your chameleon is initially going to see you as a predator and a threat. Sometimes these creatures don't like to eat if they think they're being watched. If your chameleon freezes with its tongue sticking out of its mouth then this is a sign that it's unsure and unwilling to eat with you watching.

Don't worry if chameleon doesn't respond positively at first. It can take a very long time, but stick to the same routine every day, trying to get a little closer each time but remembering to always pull away at the first sign of fear. The last thing you want is to cause your chameleon unnecessary stress. Eventually your chameleon should just snap food out of your hand.

A note of caution here – hand feeding should only be used as a way of taming and bonding, not for primary feeding. You should only hand feed a few food items each day. The rest of your chameleon's food should be given in feeder cups or roaming free in the enclosure for them to hunt.

Once they've started eating from your hand and seem confident and happy to do this, you could try putting some food on your arm to coax them to climb. Remember they will be nervous when they first do this, so try not to move at all. It is very important that you stay close to the cage so that they know they can escape back to familiar territory whenever they want to. They tend to walk in a fairly straight path so may walk slowly up your arm. Extend your other arm to guide them back to the cage.

Whenever your chameleon is on your arm or hand you will need to try and keep your face at a distance and hold your chameleon slightly higher than eye level if possible. Every time they climb onto your arm willingly don't forget to give them a treat to reinforce this behavior.

Free Ranging

Once your chameleon is used to hand feeding without trying to run and hide you can try to 'free range' them. To do this, tie one end of a bendy vine to one of the upper branches of the cage and the other end to a fake tree or climbable area a few feet away from the cage. Then, very slowly open the door and hand feed to encourage them forward, then step back, letting your chameleon find his own way out.

At first they may be reluctant to leave but eventually they should venture out, although it may take a few attempts – don't expect them to come running out excitedly as soon as you open the door.

Once they seem comfortable, hand feed them, but now of course you can get closer as they are out of the cage. Again, don't move too fast and no sudden, jerky movements. You want your chameleon to show interest when you're offering the food by touching or smelling your finger. Flatten your hand and offer a worm (or whatever their favorite treat is) so that they have to climb onto your fingers.

As mentioned earlier, chameleons don't like anything in their environment to change so when you're free ranging keep everything exactly the same. If they have a vine to climb, always make sure this is in the same position and develop a daily routine that is the same each time.

As your chameleon gets used to you, try to gently touch their nose or head every day if they let you. You may find that your Panther chameleon won't go back into their cage by themselves after free ranging and this is the time when you will most likely be able to pick them up and handle them, especially if they've been without a heat source for a while.

To return them to their cage, flatten your hand directly in front of them. It is important that your chameleon can see this. Gently nudge your hand underneath the chameleon so that they grasp it, one foot at a time. Use your other hand to gently guide them forwards. Once on your hand, slowly return them to their home. Never put your chameleon close to your face, as it may get scared and jump off, which can lead to injury. Your chameleon may gape and get huffy but if you've managed to get them to this stage then they probably won't bite so don't panic. Move very slowly and calmly. Eventually you may be able to try and gently stroke their leg or chin with the tip of your finger.

Outdoors
Although your Panther chameleon can be kept indoors for the whole of their life, it does do them good to go outside every now and then

74

in order to get unfiltered natural sunlight. There are three ways to do this; you can build an outdoor enclosure, carry them outside in a cage, or free range them and there are advantages and disadvantages to each.

Outdoor Enclosure

Of course this is a great solution but you need to decide whether you would keep your chameleon outdoors all the time or just every now and again. Keeping them outdoors forever and never bringing them inside has its advantages – you could probably keep your insects outdoors too and there is no risk of any creepy crawlies escaping into your home should they manage to get out of the cage before they're eaten. Depending on the climate you live in, you may not need heat lamps or any of that equipment because the Panther chameleon will be getting real sunlight and absorbing D3 from this source, which means you can reduce or possibly even get rid of some, if not all, of your calcium supplements. No worrying about turning the lights out, they will be ruled by nature and day and night cycles will be natural. Your cage can be as large as your garden allows, as your Panther chameleon is an arboreal creature.

Of course realistically this isn't always do-able. You need to think about the environment that you live in. If you are in England where it rains a lot, your chameleon is most likely to end up in a cage that is constantly wet. If you're in a hot country you may find that they are getting too much heat and sunlight (although this can be counteracted by misting more often and providing more plants to give them shelter from the sun). Humidity is another factor. As is cleaning the enclosure – yes it would be amazing to have an enclosure that is huge but how long will it take to clean it and is there a risk of insects hiding and not being eaten because your chameleon can't find them?

There's also the worry that your chameleon will be constantly stressed if you live in a noisy environment with neighbors' kids yelling or loud traffic noises. Add to this the risk that they may be eaten by the neighborhood cat or a passing fox and outdoor living may not be all it's cracked up to be.

Small Cage Carried Outdoors
I'm hoping your Panther chameleon's cage is too tall to be transported about, although some screen cages are incredibly light so it could be do-able. Temporarily you could house them somewhere smaller where they can sit outside and get sunlight or you could have a permanent outdoor cage that you put them in to get sunlight before bringing them back outdoors.

If you do have a temporary house to take your chameleon outdoors then of course this would need to have a mesh top or some sort of material that allows the sunlight through. You don't want them in an all glass enclosure where your chameleon will cook if you live in a hot environment. It still needs plants and branches as well in order to allow them to escape the sunlight when they get too hot and preferably tall so they can climb. Meeting all your chameleon's needs may not be doable in a small, transportable cage. Some people do take them outside like this, but you may be hindering your chameleon's health rather than helping and it needs to be thought through.

Outdoor Free-ranging
A lot of owners do this and it is successful. Your Panther chameleon gets direct sunlight without a cage or screen filtering it first. This is perfect for increasing their Vitamin D3 levels plus they will get much needed exercise, as they'll most likely explore the new area. You will need to make sure your garden has trees or bushes though because again, when they get hot they will need to shelter underneath in order to regulate their body temperatures. They won't

want to be exposed to predators, so foliage will make them feel secure. Once you are able to handle your Panther chameleon, it would be a great idea to carry them outside and place them on a low branch of a tree or on a bush. Using the same bush or tree each time means your chameleon will get used to being there and will settle easier.

A word of warning here though: if you do take your chameleon outside and they're not in an enclosure, keep an eye on them at all times. Whilst these creatures may mainly seem lumbering and slow, they can be quick and easy to lose. If you have a lot of foliage about they can become camouflaged or worse – without someone carefully watching over them, they can easily be carried off by a bird or other predator. I've heard so many stories about people who have put their chameleon on the lawn, run inside for a few minutes only to return and find their chameleon is no longer visible. It's a sad story but the moral is – don't leave your chameleon exposed outdoors. Of course, you may not have the time to just sit outdoors with them in which case, again, a cage is a safer option and free ranging should be left for a time when you are able to sit and watch them.

Tracking

There are lots of people out there saying, "Help, I've lost my chameleon!" Often it's in the cage and their enclosures are set up so perfectly they cannot find them because the chameleon is hiding away for a while after basking until its temperature has cooled back down. If you know it's inside its home, although it can be frustrating if you want to see them all the time, it's actually a good thing because it means your chameleon feels secure and you know it's safe. Eventually they will make themselves visible again.

However, sometimes people free range their Panther chameleons outside without supervision believing that their bright colors will make them easy to find again, only to discover when they return that

77

their pet has disappeared completely. This can be devastating. They will run around in a panic, searching and worrying. Sometimes they find them, sadly often they don't. This leads to people asking whether it is possible to put a tracking device on a chameleon.

There are two types of tracker you can get for pets, one is micro-chipping where a small chip is injected into the animal's skin. If ever it gets lost it only needs to be taken to a vet who will scan it and check it against the database to find out who it belongs to. It works for bigger animals but for a chameleon? Sadly it's just not possible.

These creatures are just too sensitive and fragile and the whole process of microchipping would be too traumatizing. Even if we could get a chip into them, realistically, who is going to be taking a Panther chameleon that's roaming in the bushes to the vet? Often people won't recognize them, yes they may identify it as a lizard but if you live somewhere where creatures that look similar to chameleons live in the wild, people won't always assume it's a beloved pet. Even if they did, how would they capture something that's aggressive and dislikes even its caring owner? Your Panther chameleon isn't going to walk up to them and happily climb into a box - it is going to blow itself up, hiss, run away or maybe bite if they get close enough. Therefore microchipping isn't the answer.

The other types of tracking device for pets that are available on the market are small, medallion-type objects, about the size of a coin. When the animal goes missing you can locate it using your smartphone or similar device and it will ring audibly or display on a map using GPS signals so you can find it easily.

I see two problems with these devices with regards to chameleons – one is that even the tiniest of these objects are most likely going to be too big for it. I can't see it being very easy to attach it nor can I see this happening without causing stress to the majority of these creatures. The second problem is that GPS tracking, as great as it is, isn't always accurate, so if your chameleon is just in a bush in your garden it may display a map of your area but I doubt it will pinpoint the exact bush or tree your chameleon is sat in. You still have the problem of finding it when it's camouflaged.

The bad news therefore is that there isn't a tracker available on the market at the moment for chameleons. I can give you this piece of advice though - should you lose your chameleon outside, look high up. Think about how Panther chameleons will act in the wild. Arboreal creatures will always try to climb, as this is a natural instinct and they also like the sun, so look around for suitable spots that your lizard may have tried to climb in order to reach sunlight.

If you haven't found your chameleon by nightfall don't give up. Someone once gave me this helpful tip – get a torch and search in the garden when it gets dark. Sleeping chameleons are relatively easy to spot at night because their skin becomes paler, contrasting with the darker leaves of the shrubs. Therefore it is often easier to find them in the dark.

Chapter 9: Medical Problems

A lot of illnesses in these creatures can be avoided and the majority of medical problems arise because people buy a chameleon without understanding their basic needs, their life in the wild or how to create the optimum environment. That's not to say that they will never get sick or that you're a bad owner if they do, just that if you keep these creatures in an optimal environment, feed and water them correctly and understand about temperatures, heating and lighting, et cetera than you have a better chance at keeping your pet healthy for a longer period of time as some medical problems can be avoided. Owners often don't recognise the signs or symptoms of illness and diagnosing is very difficult because, as I've mentioned previously, these lizards are wild animals and are very adept at hiding any medical issues as this would be seen as a weakness in the wild making them easy prey. As such, by the time your chameleon displays any symptoms they may in actual fact have been ill for a very long time.

Parasites

It is normal for any type of chameleon to carry a few parasites, most wild creatures do and as they are also found in their feeder insects then it's unrealistic to think otherwise but if they are out of control it could lead to extra stress or illness. If your chameleon is healthy and is kept at an optimal weight then you may never see any signs of them.

There are different types of parasites, many of which are invisible to the naked eye so it is important to take your chameleon for a vet check once a year and this should include faecal tests to check for gastrointestinal parasites as testing and treatment can eliminate them before they become a problem. You can collect fresh faecal matter – both the whitish urate and the brownish excrement – in a plastic or glass container which should then be placed in a bag to prevent desiccation. Remember to wash your hands thoroughly afterward.

Cause – Can be contracted through food and through poor hygiene levels.

Symptoms – Symptoms include failure to grow, loss of appetite, lethargy, abnormal stools, sickness, visible signs of worms, weakness, dehydration, eyes closed and vomiting.

Prevention - Prevention is often better than cure because some parasites such as Protozoa are difficult to treat. To keep parasites at bay it is important to make sure your chameleon's cage is ventilated and that you maintain a high level of hygiene. You also need to do this with the insects you keep for food so as well as spot cleaning your chameleon's enclosure daily to ensure parasites can't breed you should also spot clean the insects' environment too. Although insects you buy can contain parasites, the risk is a lot lower so try to use these instead of feeding your chameleon wild insects or vegetation or even better, breed your own.
Regular vet checks can also help to catch these parasites early before they cause serious illness.

Wild caught chameleons usually harbour parasites even when they're labelled parasite free, so this is another reason to buy captivity bred animals.

Constipation/Digestion Problems
Cause – Chameleons will often consume other materials along with their food. Usually this will pass normally but occasionally it can cause a blockage. The wrong temperature and lack of hydration can also cause digestion problems or a female may suffer with this when she has eggs.

Symptoms – Hanging over a branch and straining with nothing coming out. This can cause a prolapse.

Prevention - You can minimise this by not using substrate, keeping an eye on temperature levels and making sure your chameleon is basking throughout the day. Keep a close eye on their diet and environment and make a note of everything you feed, everything they eat and record the temperature and humidity levels. Keep them well misted and hydrated. For females, ensure there is an adequate laying bin.

Kidney Failure and Gout

Causes - Gout is when an excess of uric acids is produced in the blood. This is often caused by long-term dehydration or certain vet prescribed antibiotics.

Symptoms - It is a very complicated disease which has many symptoms and many forms including excessive drinking, not eating, reduced mobility, swelling and pain when walking or climbing and extremely aggressive behaviour (especially when joints are touched).

Prevention - It is a common cause of death in pet chameleons because low level dehydration is easy to miss. That is why it's really important to have the appropriate humidity levels as well as an effective water drip system combined with misting, as this should keep your chameleon properly hydrated. If you suspect your chameleon has gout then take them straight to the vet.

Stress

Chameleons are prone to stress especially in captivity where they only have a small environment and could be in a house not only with humans but other pets as well. Everything in your house, including you, will be viewed as a threat to your chameleon.

Causes – Poor or too much lighting, too much traffic in the household, dramatic environment changes, loud noises, other animals (including those of its own species) seeing it's reflection, poor handling (or handling or any sort) and being sprayed with cold water to name but a few. There are many more but the list is far too long to include here – basically anything can (and probably will) spook your chameleon.

Symptoms - Dramatic or dark colour changes, smelly or watery faeces, abnormally aggressive, different body temperatures, rocking, flattening its body, loss of appetite and excessive hiding amongst foliage.

Prevention – Make sure that the environment is quiet as much as possible and try to put their enclosure in an area of the house where people won't be constantly walking around. Keep other pets as far away as possible and don't ever let them near your chameleon and house other chameleons out of sight of each other. Don't put any mirrors in or near their cage so they don't ever see their reflection as they will mistake this for another chameleon. For wild caught animals make sure they are in a large environment with lots of hiding places that is as natural as possible.

Edema

This is an accumulation of excess fluids on the subcutaneous layer of the skin which causes swelling.

Causes - There are many causes but the main ones are being fed crickets or other feeders coated in excess vitamins or being in an enclosure that is too humid.

Symptoms – It is characterised by swelling that resembles a goitre in chest, throat and neck. Even pets that have lived in the same enclosure for a long time can develop symptoms so it is important that you closely monitor your pet and look for anything unusual.

Prevention – Avoid feeding on food that is gut loaded with too many vitamins and over supplementing. Avoid products that contain high levels of protein. Although gut-loading and supplementation is good for them it needs to be done in moderation, if unsure consult a vet. Also maintain good humidity levels and check these on a regular basis.

Upper Respiratory Infections

These are common in chameleons in captivity and are infections in the respiratory tract or the lungs (known as Pneumonia). If caught early enough they can be handled successfully.

Causes – The main causes are environmental contamination, poor care and husbandry issues.

Symptoms – Gaped mouth, too much mucus, inflammation, wheezing or popping sounds, or bubbling around the mouth and nose.

Prevention – Check for air quality and proper temperature of the enclosure regularly. Do a daily spot clean removing any litter including uneaten food and ensure you have good drainage as insect cultures and dirty water can increase the risk. Do a thorough clean at least once a month.

A tip to check for respiratory problems is to hold your chameleon close you your ear and listen. If you can hear creaking noises than it is suffering from a respiratory problem. Steamy showers or a warm mist humidifier can help with these problems but you will need to see a vet.

Calcium Deficiency

Calcium is used to flex muscles. If there isn't enough calcium present the animal with draw it from the calcium stored in its bones making them weak and prone to fractures.

Causes – This is caused by an insufficient lack of calcium and Vitamin A or too much phosphorous.

Symptoms – These include soft bones, soft jaw, lack of appetite, lethargy and deformities in the spine and legs.

Prevention – Coat feeders in the correct amount of calcium. Make sure they're lightly dusted – you should have a specific container used to dust feeders that is different to those used to gut-load and another one used to feed them to your chameleon. Gut-load feeders with healthy greens and fruits (for water) – remember whatever they eat is stored in their gut and will go into your chameleon when they eat the insects, hence the term 'gut-load'.

Vitamin A Deficiency

Vitamin A is readily available in nature and in the wild a Panther Chameleon absorbs this regularly as they will often eat insects and small lizards that contain this vitamin.

Causes - In captivity their diet consists primarily of insects that lack Vitamin A.

Symptoms – Swollen limbs, reduced growth rate, loss of appetite, skin abnormalities, swelling in the eyes, upper respiratory infections, liver enlargement and bone abnormalities.

Prevention – Provide your chameleon with the most nutritious diet by offering as wide a variety of insects as possible and research which ones are good for them. Gut-load insects with vitamin rich foods such as apple, cornmeal, carrots, legumes, sweet potatoes, oranges, etc… Coat feeders with multi-vitamin supplements containing vitamin A approximately two to three times a month.

Dehydration
Dehydration occurs when the chameleon doesn't take in enough water.

Causes – Not providing enough water through misting or drippers or not having enough adequate surfaces to collect water. In some cases it can be caused by serious internal issues.

Symptoms – Orange or yellow urate (instead of white), sunken eyes (not round and bulbous), loss of appetite and weak skin that won't revert back to normal when pulled.

Prevention – Make sure there is sufficient foliage available as this will catch the water making it easier for your chameleon to drink or to get moisture by eating the leaves. Keep an eye out to see if your chameleon is drinking falling water either from the dripper or from misting sessions. Mist regularly at a minimum of twice a day, ideally at least four times. Time how long it takes for the water to dry up as your chameleon may not have chance to drink if the cage is immediately drying out. If this is the case you will need to adjust your temperature, humidity levels and/or misting sessions.
If you see any of the symptoms listed above consult your vet immediately as dehydration can point to a serious health problem and if you know you are providing enough drinking water than it can signal an underlying cause.

Stuck Shed
Chameleons, unlike some reptiles such as snakes, don't shed their skin all in one piece but instead shed in patches. When they're ready to shed you will usually notice that they've turned an overall dull

colour and their eyelids may 'pop' making them look even more bug-eyed than usual. This usually happens every four to six weeks although some owners report that their chameleons shed less often once they are adults. It happens because the body grows a new layer of skin which starts to separate from the old. A thin layer of fluid forms between, pushing the old layer of skin away from the body.

Causes – If the enclosure is too dry, fluid won't be able to form between the old and new layer of skin and the lizard can't shed it.

Symptoms – Usually you will see large pieces of shedded skin stuck the chameleon's body, often around the eyes, tail and head.

Prevention – DO NOT PEEL any skin that you see as this is not only dangerous but painful. If it is stuck to the chameleon it means it is not ready to come off yet. Your chameleon may seem itchy and grumpy so you can make it easier by spraying your chameleon with water and, if they allow it, gently massaging its skin until it starts to peel off. Stuck shed rarely happens in the wild because it is a more naturally humid environment that these creatures live in. If your conditions are optimal then you may not even notice that your chameleon has shed its skin because in ideal conditions shedding happens quicker and often they eat it afterwards. To prevent stuck shed you need to make sure your enclosure has the correct humidity levels and that you are misting correctly and regularly. Check that the last spray of the day has completed dried before putting the lights out. If you find your enclosure is still wet at night you may need to start your final misting session earlier.
If retained shed is severe and you cannot get it off, even with the correct humidity levels and spraying you may need to see the vet.

Egg Binding/Egg Retention

This is common in reptiles and occurs when the female cannot produce mature eggs during reproduction. If not treated properly it can lead to death after a few days.

Causes – Anatomical defects, large malformed eggs, poor condition of the female, lack of a good nesting site, dehydration, improper temperatures.

Symptoms – Lethargy (even pregnant chameleons with a swollen abdomen should still remain fairly active), depression, raised hind limbs and constant straining without providing any eggs, pacing along the bottom of the cage or constantly digging without laying eggs.

Prevention – Provide a good egg laying bin where the female can dig a tunnel in which to lay her eggs. Feed gravid females a nutritious diet with additional supplementation – sometimes you may need to hand feed if your chameleon looks exhausted. Mist regularly, this may be need more often than normal to prevent dehydration, especially if she is digging a lot.

Bodily Injuries

These include injuries, cuts and scrapes. It is important to treat any cuts and scrapes no matter how minor they look to prevent infections. Large lesions or serious injuries may need the vet to attend to them to prevent septic wounds.

Causes – These can be caused by regular play or something more serious such as a falling bulb or the enclosure being knocked over, your chameleon being dropped when handled or being attacked by another chameleon or other animal. Can also be caused by too much stress – if your chameleon has seen another of its kind, for example, it can cause itself injury during its display of aggression.

Symptoms – As these are physical they're fairly easily identified. Watch your pet closely to see if it's in pain. Periodically examine it for cuts or scrapes. If your chameleon has suffered a major injury they may have large lesions or a limp.

Prevention – Careful handling at all times. Leave their home undisturbed and avoid moving it, ensure that children and other animals are kept away so they don't knock the enclosure over. House only one chameleon to a cage, out of sight of others.

Mouth Issues
Causes – Poor nutrition or husbandry, overcrowded cage, poor temperature regulation, improper phosphorous levels, vitamin deficiency, insufficient calcium levels and scratches or wounds to the mouth.

Symptoms – Brownish yellow matter or stains surrounding the teeth and gums. Swelling of the lower jaw or dehydrated matter around the mouth. If left untreated it can cause loss of appetite.

Prevention – Provide your chameleon with the proper nutrition it requires. Watch carefully and make sure there is nothing in the enclosure that they can eat which will damage their mouth.

Tongue Problems
Causes – Mouth infection, vitamin deficiency, muscular problem or physical damage or injury.

Symptoms – Failure to remove tongue when feeding, swollen gular area, swelling of the tongue or inability to put tongue back in their mouth. If the latter happens it is important to ensure the tongue remains moist. Another, very serious symptom is the failure to use the tongue at all to feed.

Prevention – Provide a good nutritious diet of a variety of insects which have been gut loaded 18-24 hours before being fed to your chameleon and ensure your chameleon cannot injure or do any physical damage to its tongue in the cage.

Thermal Burns
Cause – The lamp is too close to a branch putting it within reach of the chameleon.

Symptoms – Light green patch of skin, with or without blisters which then turns black leaving a raw area that is prone to infection.

Prevention – Place your basking light at least 30 centimetres (12 inches) away from your chameleon and make sure there are no branches or vines near the light. Remember your chameleon can (and will) climb the cage walls or ceilings, their aim is to get as close to the light as possible regardless of whether they get burnt or not. If you do notice any burns you need to seek treatment from a vet immediately as your chameleon will most likely need antibiotics. The vet will also give you a cream to soothe the exposed area and prevent infection.

Metabolic Bone Disease
This is probably the top cause of growth defects and deaths in these animals. It is a very slow and painful killer yet a lot of the time it can be prevented.

Causes –This is usually a dietary deficiency or lack of ultraviolet light.

Symptoms – Early signs include the softening of bones, swollen joints, clumsiness, rubbery jaw and bowed legs. Advanced signs include tremors, broken bones, general weakness, anorexia, difficulty projecting tongue and trouble climbing.

Prevention – Chameleons need at least 12 hours of UVB light daily in order to properly process calcium from food. Being outside in unfiltered sunlight is the best but indoor bulbs are sufficient. Regular vet visits are also needed so that any signs can be spotted early.

These are the main diseases that appear in chameleons. Although the majority of symptoms are listed for each case your chameleon may display others.

Unlike a dog, your pet chameleon isn't going to be able to whine or bark to alert you to pain or illness, therefore you need to give your chameleon a health check regularly and be attentive to warning signs. The following is a check list of what you should be looking for:

- Any bodily injuries
- Sunken eyes
- Respiration difficulties or infections
- Excess mucus
- Foaming at the mouth
- Visible signs of stress such as abnormally dark colours with no apparent reason
- Restlessness or roaming around the bottom of their cage
- Difficulty walking
- Limited or no climbing

Please don't try and play vet – if your chameleon shows any of the signs of illness that are listed here or elsewhere in the book you need to take them to a vet, preferably one who specialises in Panther Chameleons or at the very least reptiles in order to get professional advice and treatment.

Chapter 10: Breeding

Chameleons of any breed are notorious for having short life spans in captivity. Before the 90's it was pretty much impossible to keep them alive for more than a year or so never mind breed them in captivity. Thanks to the Internet and those with advanced knowledge educating new owners, it is now possible to breed and raise these creatures successfully and over the last two decades chameleon care has improved astronomically. Several species, including the Panther chameleon, have stable, captive-bred populations and with proper husbandry and care these beautiful lizards can have a longer lifespan than ever before.

Some chameleon owners breed their Panther chameleons as a way of extending their interest in husbandry techniques. Whilst it can be challenging, it is possible to successfully breed and raise these creatures as long as the person doing so has good knowledge of reproduction in Panther chameleons as well as the suitable equipment required for each stage of the process. That being said, I would never recommend that you breed any type of chameleon as a novice and it should only really be attempted when you have many years' experience caring for these creatures as well as other reptiles.

Why Breed?

There is a difference between breeding to raise babies and breeding to sell. However, breeding is still breeding, no matter what your motives you will still end up with a clutch of Panther chameleons. As far as I can tell there are around six main reasons why people choose to breed.

More Chameleons

If you've got this far into the book then you know that raising a Panther chameleon isn't cheap or easy yet people still keep them. Whatever it is they can be strangely addictive and once you have one you may find you want more and more. You may start with a male then add a female to your collection then you may have fantasies of breeding them, keeping a few and selling the rest. However, whilst you may have enough love for twenty or thirty, do you have the resources? Whilst we will go into this in more detail later on, I will say that if your motivation to breed is because you want more chameleons then don't do it. Why can't you just add to your collection one chameleon at a time? Trust me, the cost of buying and setting up one chameleon a year is a lot less than setting up and raising ten or twenty baby chameleons or more all at the same time for at least three months or longer. Concentrating on the husbandry of a few animals will also ensure that it is still fun and won't take all your waking hours to care for them. More chameleons doesn't necessarily mean more enjoyment, in fact the opposite is often the case, as it can cause more stress for both you and the hatchlings.

Fun And Experience

In my opinion there is no better reason to breed your Panther chameleons. If these are the only reasons you're doing it then you are not going to worry about getting your investment back, instead it's just another facet of your hobby. It is also the best way to ensure your chameleons are well looked after because you are more likely to prepare for breeding slowly and over time, investigating and researching how to do it properly and concentrating on just one clutch. If you truly love chameleons then there is nothing more special and exciting than seeing one hatch for yourself. It is a truly amazing feeling. Those who breed for fun are actually going to be better breeders because they will be thinking about how to properly take care of the animals rather than turning their females into egg factories and selling the offspring off too early in a desperate bid to make a profit. Of course you're going to have to sell off most, if not all, of your babies; it's not realistic to think that you can raise a whole clutch of chameleons for the next eight years nor can you just release them into the wild (they would not survive!)

Because You Think You Have To
There is so much misleading information out there about chameleons but even more so when it comes to egg laying. Some of it causes people to panic and I believe one of these myths – that your female will die egg bound if she's not mated – is a reason why people breed without thinking of the consequences. As mentioned earlier, egg binding is when the female retains her eggs, however it has nothing to do with being mated or not. She can still become egg bound after being bred.

To Save The Wild Chameleons
There is a market out there where people are capturing wild chameleons and selling them to people who are desperate for these pets. This causes worry over the population of chameleons going extinct, so of course, a solution is for people to breed more chameleons so that people will buy them from a sustainable source and won't buy wild caught ones. What's more, if nobody sells these animals then of course they can be shipped off to a country where they can be released back into the wild – extinction problem solved! What more noble a reason can there be to breed? However, at the risk of sounding sarcastic and mean, this is just a dream, they'd never survive and even if they did it would have to be done as part of a proper re-introduction program, which means they would be taken from professional, expert breeders, not those that are small-scale doing it from their own homes.

Attention And Status
In some circles, being a chameleon breeder is a status symbol. You hear breeders being talked about as if they are the experts on all things related to these lizards and sometimes this might be the case.

However, in order to be this great revered fountain of knowledge you need to have that experience and that means raising these creatures successfully for many years, first as an owner, then as a breeder, so you need to know what you're doing.

Money

I have to add it in here, we will discuss it further down as well but of course money is going to be the main reason for a lot of people to breed. It should really have been top of the list. Who doesn't want to make money doing something they love? However, it's not as easy as hatching a clutch of Panther chameleons and putting them on the Internet. I'm not saying this can't be done, but there are all sorts of factors to take into consideration. Are you going to just raise a few clutches to enhance your hobby and see what breeding is all about, making money as a side line because you need to sell them or are you going to set up a serious business?

One thing you don't want to do is to breed them, not sell them and have to sell them off cheap in order to get rid of them. This won't make you money (or at least not a decent amount) nor will it do any good for the Panther chameleons themselves, as you risk selling them as cheap pets to people who will balk at finding out that a creature they paid £35 for costs £1000 or more to feed and house.

The Breeding Process

Okay so you want to breed, maybe for one of the reasons named above, maybe for your own reason but remember one thing - only healthy animals should be bred. In captivity, a female can produce between 10-40 eggs, although 20 is about average, multiple times per year which means very few animals are needed to maintain a productive breeding colony. A responsible breeder will only breed the same female once or twice a year and if you keep her at a healthy weight she shouldn't lay as many clutches anyway. There are some irresponsible breeders out there who will breed the same female four times a year, which can lead to poor health and a shorter lifespan.

Choosing Your Chameleons

If you are buying a pair to mate then it is advisable that you buy a juvenile pair and raise them until adults before breeding. This is because if you buy two adults to breed (or you have one adult already and buy another) you can never be sure how old the adult that you purchased is and may find that they're already too old to breed. By raising them yourself from juvenile you know they have been given the correct care and nutrition to ensure they are healthy enough to breed.

A lot of breeders prefer to keep the lines pure whereas others experiment with 'crosses'. A 'cross' or a 'morph' is when two Panther chameleons from two different locales are bred so, for instance, a Nosy Be might be bred with a Nosy Faly or an Ambilobe. As they are all compatible, this is at the discretion of the breeder.

In-breeding is a separate matter and this is when two related chameleons are bred. Whilst there isn't enough scientific evidence that says inbreeding affects the general health of chameleons, and it is done by some breeders, I wouldn't recommend it because there is always a chance that, as with any animal, it could lead to unhealthy babies.

Once you have chosen your chameleons, make sure they are fully-grown adults. Sexual maturity in females is dependent upon size and those that grow quickly can lay fertile eggs before they are around six months old, although seven to eleven months is more common. Males take longer to mature and are usually ready to mate at around nine to twelve months.

However, it is dangerous to have a sub-adult female lay eggs, as their bodies are still trying to grow. Forcing her to gestate and lay a clutch is very demanding and will take the majority of her energy; doing this before they're ready will shorten their life. As with everything else related to these delicate creatures, patience is a virtue.

Breeding

Of course you are going to have to put a pair of Panther chameleons together in order to mate, but until you are ready to do so you should always keep them in separate cages and out of sight from each other, only putting them together for a short time in order for the breeding process to take place. In the wild they wouldn't live together, as they are solitary creatures, so keeping them housed together indefinitely for breeding purposes will only cause them both stress and shorten their lifespans.

A peach/pink colored female is usually receptive for mating, so when you think your female is going to be ready place the two chameleons in the same cage. You can put a male into the female cage and this has been done successfully, but there is a theory that if you place a female into a male's territory he'll be more aggressive and therefore breed with her in order to establish dominance.

Whichever way you do it, it is important that as soon as you introduce them, you closely monitor the female over the next several seconds. Mating will only be successful if she's ovulating, so focus on her reaction to the male. Once she spots the male, she will either calmly walk away, which is a sign that she is receptive, or she will become defensive; widening her body whilst hissing or may try to run away (or in some cases do both). These are signs that she isn't ready, so if she appears distressed then remove her immediately.

If your female is receptive then you can leave the pair together and allow nature to take its course. Mating should last anywhere from five to thirty minutes, but as it can take place more than once, most breeders leave the chameleons together for around twelve to twenty four hours before putting them back in their separate cages.

Conveniently, your female chameleon will tell her owner if she is pregnant (or gravid) by changing to a dark brown color with a bright peach stripe down each of her sides.

The gestation period (the time between mating and egg laying) is usually around three to four weeks, although sometimes it can be up to five to six weeks. During this time, feed your female as much food as she will eat, making sure to dust the feeders once or twice a week with a high quality calcium supplement. You should already have an egg-laying bin in the bottom of her cage but if not, now is the time to set one up. Once you see your female pacing around the bottom of her cage, place her in the egg-laying bin, as this is a sign that she's ready to lay her eggs.

This is a difficult time for you as a breeder because although you need to know where she lays her eggs, it is important that she doesn't catch sight of you watching her because she could become egg bound if she feels too insecure to lay them. She may dig a couple of holes until she finds a spot she likes, then will dig a tunnel that is around six to eight inches deep.

Your female will be exhausted and often dehydrated once she has finished laying, so should be put in a quiet place with a slow dripper. You can mist if you think it's necessary but only do a short session and spray the leaves around her rather than the female chameleon, as she will simply want to rest. You can put some feeder insects in too, as she may want to feed, but don't put in too many crickets as the last thing you want to do is annoy her if she just wants to drink rather than eat.

One point to make here is that your Panther chameleon can retain sperm, which means she can lay another fertilized clutch a few months after the first despite not being mated again. This is a factor that needs to be considered when you are deciding whether you have the space and resources to raise baby chameleons.

Incubation

The eggs should be dug up and artificially incubated. This is because if you leave them where they are it is difficult to get the temperature and the moisture levels right, so many may not hatch at all.

Mostly, female chameleons will dig a tunnel in the corner of the bin and lay them somewhere near the bottom of the bin in a tightly packed ball, so you need to dig slowly and carefully when searching for eggs. This can take a very long time, especially if the egg-laying bin is large. Don't become discouraged if you cannot find any immediately. It is a delicate and often time-consuming process, even for a seasoned breeder.

The best way to dig up eggs is to move your fingertips back and forth as if you're brushing dust or sand from an object. Do not use a tool, otherwise you will lose the sensitivity of touch and could damage the eggs. Although they will usually be laid in a clump, the eggs shouldn't be stuck together. Eggs that are fertile are white in color and, if illuminated from behind in a dark room, will have visible blood vessels.

Once you have found them, carefully remove one egg at a time and place them in an incubation container. As they don't require large amounts of oxygen, a plastic container with a tight-fitting lid is usually a suitable incubator. Some chameleon eggs require air holes to be drilled into the box but successful breeders of Panther chameleons have found that air holes aren't necessary and can dry the substrate out. As they are usually buried six or more inches into the earth in the wild, these air holes shouldn't be needed.

You will need to use a substrate that is absorbent and won't mold easily but that allows oxygen to reach the eggs. Although you can use the same peat/soil and sand mix that you use in the egg-laying bin, a lot of breeders will recommend using vermiculate or perlite because it is cleaner. Both are made from volcanic rock heated to high temperatures to make them expand and become absorbent but as they are mineral based, neither will mold unless they become contaminated. Some breeders prefer vermiculite, as they believe it to be more resistant to mold growth, whilst others claim perlite is more open and has better airflow. There is evidence to show that both these materials have been used successfully and are used in much the same way, so whichever you choose is entirely up to you.

A good way to ensure you have enough water to substrate ratio is to weigh them both, then mix together in a plastic bag. Start with the dry material first. You will need enough to cover the bottom of the incubation box and the depth should be the size of the eggs, although I would always use slightly more to be certain you have enough. The water content needs to be twice the weight of the dry material, so for example, if you use 75g of substrate then you need 150g of water.

The dry substance and the water need to be mixed together thoroughly so the water is distributed evenly, which is why a plastic bag is handy as you can gather the top and shake it. To test the moisture levels, squeeze a handful in your fist. You shouldn't be able to squeeze more than a couple of drops of water out and it should retain its shape when you open your hand. If you are worried about not getting the water content correct you can buy a specialist substrate such as Hatchright, which is already at the correct moisture level.

Place the damp material into the incubation box. Don't press it down but use your finger to make a hole large enough to hold each egg. If possible, the eggs should be separated and spaced at least one inch apart. Not only does this prevent premature hatching, but also means that if one goes bad the others should still be okay.

Unlike bird eggs that keep the embryo the right way up even when the egg is moved, the embryo in reptile eggs sink to the bottom in the first few days, then an air sack will form at the top of the egg, meaning that if the egg is turned the embryo inside will die. It is very important therefore that you carefully lift the eggs from the egg-nesting site and place them exactly the same way into the holes you have made in the incubator box. Bury with around thirty percent of them sticking out of the surface so they can get oxygen. When finished, place the lid on the box and they are ready to incubate.

Panther chameleon eggs take a long time to incubate and this incubation period can drastically vary. Some eggs can hatch within six months whilst others can take anywhere between twelve and fourteen months, so breeders need to be patient.

There are two ways to incubate Panther chameleon eggs. The first – and easiest – way is to keep them at a constant temperature between 22-25 degrees Celsius (72-78 degrees Fahrenheit). The other option is to incubate the eggs at varying temperatures. It is thought that Panther chameleon eggs go through a period of diapause or non-development and varying the temperatures at which they're incubated can shorten this non-development period, which means they will hatch sooner. Breeders therefore will incubate the eggs at around 24 degrees Celsius (around 75-78 degrees Fahrenheit) for the first three to four weeks, reduce this to 18-21 degrees Celsius (65-70 degrees Fahrenheit) for six to eight weeks and then raise them back to around 24 degrees Celsius (75-78 degrees Fahrenheit) for the remainder of the incubation period. Eggs kept this way can hatch as early as five months.

The problem with increasing and decreasing the temperature is that if done incorrectly it can prevent the eggs from hatching at all. Slow temperature changes shouldn't affect the Panther chameleon eggs, but fast changes do, which is why some breeders don't recommend reptile incubators, as these can experience rapid temperature fluctuations for no apparent reason.

Whilst you should resist the urge to constantly open the box to check on the eggs, as this will affect the temperature and humidity levels inside, you should open the container every few weeks for a moment or two just to allow a fresh supply of air inside. As this may reduce the humidity levels inside, you may have to re-mist the box, but avoid spraying the eggs directly.

Be patient and only throw away eggs that have gone moldy. Just before hatching, the eggs will form small beads of water on their surface, which looks as a bit like the egg is sweating, and they will also begin to cave in. This shouldn't be confused with an egg that is going bad. All it means is that the young lizard is preparing to leave its shell and within a few days they should hatch.

The Hatchling

Often babies break through the egg and remain in the same spot without moving for hours, if not days, sometimes with just their noses pushed out. Owners, especially those new to breeding, often believe that the babies are dead, when in actual fact they are simply absorbing whatever is left of their egg yolk. Pulling or cutting them out of the egg can cause injury or can tear their umbilicus, which can in turn lead to infections. Instead just leave them where they are, once it is ready to emerge completely and face the world it will wriggle away. Sometimes the movement of newly-hatched babies may stimulate the un-hatched eggs to break open, another good reason to leave them in the incubation box. As some babies don't eat immediately after hatching it is not necessary to throw any food into the box.

Other than moving them to a smaller enclosure and feeding them small insects such as pinhead crickets and fruit flies, the husbandry for babies is pretty much the same as that of a juvenile or adult Panther chameleon, albeit with slightly different temperature and humidity levels (see Chapter Four for these temperatures). It is good to include some live plants such as Pothos in their environment, as not only will they provide hiding spots, but also the babies will eat them. It is possible to keep six or seven hatchlings in one enclosure as long as you provide enough food for all. It is not recommended that you keep the whole clutch together, as they will be constantly competing for resources. As baby Panther chameleons will eat a lot, you should provide a large amount of pinhead crickets that are dusted with calcium powder each day as well as fruit flies. Putting food in their cage two or three times a day is the best way to ensure they all get plenty of food.

Make sure you mist in order to provide drinking water and to raise the relative humidity but take care not to drown them. Gently spray the leaves around them rather than the babies themselves. Check that their urate is white; orange urate can signal dehydration.

By three months the babies should be well established and ready to go to new homes. By this point it needs to be one chameleon per enclosure.

Where To Sell

You may be wondering how and where you can sell your Panther chameleons. In this day and age you are lucky, because thanks to technology it is easier to connect with people and find those who want to buy a chameleon, whether that is through an intermediary or directly to customers themselves.

As I've said before, don't sell before three months because this marks an age where the baby is big enough to handle being transferred to a new home and will have established a good track record of eating and drinking.

Wholesalers

For breeders who want to make money, landing a wholesaler is the dream, as they will buy in bulk and in turn sell them to various retail outlets. This means they could in fact buy whole clutches and if you have a good relationship with them then this means you could in fact sell every single chameleon you ever hatch and it is quick and simple.

Before you say "sign me up", remember that you may not make a huge profit; usually a wholesaler will negotiate a deal that could be twenty five percent of the retail price, so if this is £250, they could realistically pay £62.50 for each Panther chameleon. For thirty therefore you would get £1875. Therefore to make serious money you would need your females to lay large clutches as many times as possible and breed her each time, which of course isn't healthy for your Panther chameleon and will shorten their lifespan. Of course if you have many females it may be easier and put less strain on each but still don't expect to recover all your costs and of course, those females that lay huge clutches are usually overfed and unhealthy so you are at risk of just breeding to make money without thinking about your Panther chameleon's wellbeing.

Another disadvantage is, of course, you don't know who is going to get your baby chameleons – are they going to be sold to responsible owners or people who buy them on a whim and then can't take care of them? Do you even care? (If the answer to this last question is no, then I urge you not to breed at all!)

If this is a route you want to take you can often find wholesalers advertising in the back of trade magazines or on the Internet, usually attached to sites dedicated to reptiles and even specifically chameleons. Usually their adverts will state that they don't sell to the public. Some may also be asking for whole clutches of captive-bred chameleons, as they know these are better than wild caught.

Retail Outlets

Unlike wholesalers who sell to outlets, a retail outlet is the business that sells to the general public such as pet stores or sales websites. The upside of selling direct to these retailers is that you can negotiate a higher profit, sometimes 50% of the retail price. That means if they are going to sell for £250, you can ask for £125 for each chameleon. If you have thirty, that gives you £3750 back, assuming you sell the whole clutch.

The other advantage is that you can get an idea of who the end buyer will be and how your chameleons will be treated. If you sell to a pet shop who you know has one or two fish tanks in which they keep all their chameleons with a bowl of water in the corner, then you can bet that your babies won't have a long or happy life. If you sell to those who specialize in exotic pets however, it is often fair to assume that they will give good advice to the end buyer and your chameleons will be cared for and go to good homes.

The downside is that retail outlets probably won't have the space to buy a whole clutch and therefore you may have to approach a few in order to sell all your babies.

To find respectable retail outlets search the Internet or the back of trade magazines or look for them at reptile shows. A lot of knowing who to sell to is down to experience but as a new breeder you won't have this, so try and go for those who have a good reputation. Post on forums and ask for advice from the reptile or chameleon community.

Direct Selling

This is where the serious money is. You're going to sell your Panther chameleon for £250 minimum and everyone is going to come direct to you. Yes, this is kind of the idea, you've cut out the middle man so now you can sell for a higher price and you get to see what kind of homes your babies are going to and you can pass on your own expert advice, so know that the new owners are going to be able to take care of them properly, plus you get to meet new people in the Panther chameleon community.

However, the disadvantages are not everyone is going to buy from you and you are going to have to make multiple points of sales in order to get rid of all your babies. (If you have thirty chameleons then you will need thirty customers). Not only that, but you will also have to deal with the members of the public, which means you are going to meet people who might be disagreeable and trying to take advantage of you by negotiating lower prices. You also have the added complication of shipping the chameleons as well as the risk of losing money and gaining a bad reputation should they not arrive alive at the buyers' end.

If you are letting people come to your house then you need to be prepared for anyone and any questions they may have. Do you really want a bunch of strangers coming into your home? Some of them might be great but you also have to expect people who are just coming to nosy at your set up and ask questions without purchasing.

This can be avoided by meeting in a public place with you taking photographs of the set up and the babies with you, although some people may want to see the chameleons in person.

Of course you could pack up all (or a good selection) of your Panther chameleons and display them in a trade show but the problem you'll encounter here will be the wellbeing and safety of your chameleons whilst in transit and at the shows. Again, people will try and negotiate good prices and you will be in direct competition with other breeders, some of which may be more knowledgeable and have many more years' experience than you. One thing is certain: if you are selling direct you are going to have to advertise whether this be in trade magazines or via the Internet – setting up a website or selling via social media pages. There is a lot of competition out there and you are going to need to build a reputation for yourself.

Unless you are lucky enough to live in a large city where people are willing to collect from you direct, you are going to need to become familiar with shipping and the shipping process which once again, means eating into any money you may make.

Breeders

If money isn't the reason you are breeding then you may be able to negotiate with other breeders to take your offspring to add extra blood lines to their breeding projects. Be aware that they probably won't pay a high amount as, like you, they probably aren't making a lot of (if any) money from this venture but purely doing it because it's a hobby they love. They may trade some of their own creatures for yours. You can search the Internet to find reputable breeders but try and do this in advance, as it will take time not only to find them but also to sort the good from the bad and build up solid relationships

How To Be A Responsible Breeder

You need to ensure your Panther chameleons are being kept in proper conditions. If you are breeding please make sure you:

- Only breed the healthiest animals.

- Raise babies in a way that gives them a good start in life.

- Don't sell any chameleon that you breed until it is old enough to be re-homed.

- Provide new owners with a care sheet and ensure they understand how to provide care.

- Check those buying from you have a suitable set up in advance.

- Discourage buyers who want two chameleons for breeding purposes from buying a pair that are siblings.

- Be open and honest and encourage buyers to come back to you with questions and provide them with the correct advice even after they've made a purchase.

If you are truly breeding because you love these animals and not to make quick, easy money then you should be willing to provide advice even if you know a customer may have bought a chameleon elsewhere.

Although I don't agree that a novice should breed these creatures, I do understand that breeding is a necessity because obviously there is a market for them and if nobody bred them then it would only lead to more being taken from the wild.

Chapter 11: Common Myths

Panther chameleons, despite having been kept in captivity as pets for so many years, are still greatly misunderstood. There is so much information out there that is misleading and contradictory that it's impossible to know who to believe and who to ignore. What I have noticed through both experience and research is that there are some common myths which can lead owners, especially new ones who have no other experience to compare with, to thinking they are doing the right thing yet actually damaging these delicate creatures and doing more harm than good.

Chameleons Absorb Water Through Their Skin

This frustrates me to no end. Chameleons do not like bathing. You won't go in the wild and see them rolling about in puddles of water, their tongues lolling out of their mouths like puppies. They have evolved to live in trees and they lick water droplets from leaves. They do not sit in puddles of water splashing about nor do they drink from them. Although people will say spray your chameleon directly when misting, this is just to help keep their skin moist so they can shed easier, it has nothing to do with hydration as they do not absorb water through their skin.

I would also like to point out that yes, sunken eyes are a sign of dehydration, but they can also point to other problems too. Stress, illness, parasites, infection and extreme weight loss can all cause eyes to become sunken. Rather than putting your chameleon in a bath to soak them, check your humidity and temperature levels and look at your misting techniques and the suitability of the enclosure itself. If you are certain your husbandry techniques are the best they can be then taking your pet to a vet that specializes in exotic animals for a fecal test and examination is the solution rather than a bath.

Glass And Substrate Kill

Hopefully I haven't been guilty of perpetuating this myth earlier in this book when I spoke about caging and substrate. Both of these are controversial topics, especially the latter and although I am not a fan of novice owners using them I don't want people to go off and start lecturing others for doing so. The myth that "glass and substrate will kill your chameleon" is another popular one. When owners talk about glass enclosures being suitable they're not talking about a fish tank being placed on its end and having the top covered but actual glass enclosures with a mesh or screen lid and vents at the bottom to allow air to circulate that have been designed especially for chameleons. The two are very different – a glass fish tank most likely will kill your chameleon eventually and I believe this could be where this myth began. The screen and mesh screens are most often recommended as they have the benefits of great air circulation as well as being lightweight and relatively cheap, but chameleon owners have complained that it is difficult to maintain proper humidity levels because the airflow is so good and keepers then overcompensate by misting more regularly. A glass enclosure made specifically for chameleons however will help keep humidity levels high.

And substrate? Yes it can cause impaction and I don't recommend it for novice owners but there's no denying it makes for a more natural environment. The key to avoiding impaction is keeping the chameleon in the correct environment with optimum temperature and humidity levels and a healthy diet consisting of a variety of insects and the correct amount of supplementation. That way even if your chameleon does swallow a tiny bit of soil it shouldn't cause impaction if your chameleon is healthy.

Chameleons Get Lonely

People stare into a Panther chameleon's cage and think how sad they look. "You should get it a friend" they often remark. Possibly this is helpful advice for a rabbit or a hamster or whatever likes to be around other creatures. Is it the answer for my aggressive Panther chameleon that loves his privacy? No. What people don't comprehend is that even in the wild these creatures will avoid each other. The difference is, in a wild environment they have all the space in the world to escape from one another. Each will have their own territory and they will stay separate, other than to mate. They like it this way, their lives are less stressful and that is why they live for longer.

Chameleons Love Their Owners

I'm so frustrated when I see photographs of people on the Internet with their chameleons on their shoulders or wrapped in blankets being carried out and about in public places, people fawning all over them. Not only is it perpetuating a myth but it's also cruelty in my book. I don't want to sound mean but your Panther chameleon isn't going to love you. It may climb onto your hand if you've got food – this is because you have food or it expects food! It may climb up your arm and it may allow you to hold it. This is tolerance not love. Do they enjoy it? I want to say no but some may like it, we can't be certain. What we do know is that they are wild animals, solitary in nature and prone to stress...you decide. Again, don't be fooled, a picture may paint a thousand words but in the case of Panther chameleons these words are usually misinterpreted.

I'm not saying don't ever handle your chameleon but do so in moderation. Remember their enclosure is a micro-climate ideal to them, when you take them out of it you are subjecting them to alien conditions which will take a toll on their bodies. They can handle being removed at times for short periods but remember they need the correct light, humidity and heat to thrive and they don't get this sitting on your shoulder watching TV.

Give Food And Supplements In High Amounts

Baby chameleons need to be given as much food as they will eat –
this is because they are growing and all the energy they receive from
their food will be used for these growth spurts. Adult chameleons
however will have a slower growth rate, so feeding them what they
like will only cause them to put on weight and, in females, can lead
to producing high levels of eggs, which can cause egg retention. Yes,
you may put twenty crickets in your adult chameleon's cage and said
chameleon may eat them all but remember, they are wild animals
and in the wild they would eat as many insects as they can catch
because the next day they may in fact not find any. This instinct to
eat whatever they see is still in them in captivity so it is up to you as
an owner to decide what they need and give it to them. If you gut-
load correctly, provide a mixture of different creepy crawlies and
take your Panther chameleon out into the natural sunlight every now
and again then you may need very little supplementation. When you
do supplement you need to lightly dust not coat your insects so that
they are pure white. Too much supplementation is dangerous to the
health of your chameleon. The Panther chameleons who have longer
lifespans in captivity tend to be the ones who have very little
supplements at all. With these creatures it is all about moderation
and care, it is so complicated that if you are unsure you should check
with a vet who is experienced in exotic animals, preferably with
specific knowledge about Panther chameleons.

Enclosures Need To Be Placed Near A Window

You've heard that Panther chameleons need natural sunlight so of
course why not put your cage near a window? It will also cause your
plants to grow, right? Well if the mid-morning sun shines through
the glass window the cage will act like a heat trap and basically your
chameleon will cook. UVB rays don't penetrate glass either, so it is a
redundant act. Your chameleon needs natural, unfiltered sunlight,
which means taking them outdoors and free ranging them. In winter,
cold air falling from the window onto the cage will put your Panther

chameleon at risk of a respiratory infection or will cool them so much their metabolism slows down, making it difficult for them to digest their food and creating a whole host of problems. Put your enclosure in a corner away from direct sunlight and take them outside if you want them to have natural light.

Increase Airflow By Putting Enclosure Next To A Fan
Another no, no I'm afraid. You need to create a natural environment, which means ventilation should be passive rather than forced. A fan or vent will force airflow into the cage; if you have one blowing through it all this will do is dry out the habitat, push away any humidity and eventually causes dehydration.

Misting And High Humidity Is Needed
Yes they do need this, but they don't need to be constantly wet. Too much moisture caused by over-misting is often the first thing that kills Panther chameleons in captivity. You need to hydrate your chameleon and regular misting sessions are a must, but there needs to be a balance between the two. Think how the chameleon lives in the wild – it rains and this rainfall dries up... that is the effect you want. If the environment is too humid for too long it becomes an incubation tank for bacteria, which can cause lung infections and this is exacerbated by insect debris, skin shed, decaying leaves and so on.

The problem is that no care sheet is written specifically with you and your chameleon in mind. Yes, this book is a guideline designed to point you in the right direction but you need to observe how the water behaves in your cage. If it dries up after an hour, you need to mist more, if it's still wet after three hours, mist less. Unfortunately its trial and error, which is why it's always good for you to set up the environment and have a play around with humidity and moisture before bringing your chameleon home.

Conclusion

By now you should understand that a chameleon isn't an easy pet for the lazy owner. They are wild animals whose needs are often misunderstood. If you love them and you are prepared to take care of them well then by all means get one. They are wonderful, fascinating creatures. However, if you just want a novelty pet and you aren't interested in meeting their needs, preferring instead to just put them in a small cage where you can watch them for a while, then these aren't for you at all. I think rather than looking at them as just pets we should look at them as a hobby as well. They take up time and if you don't enjoy carrying out the tasks such as misting, checking temperatures, feeding and making adjustments, then this isn't for you.

Although fairly expensive, Panther chameleons can be bred in high numbers in captivity and this can lead to 'panic selling', as there is only so long they can be housed together and of course, a high amount of babies are expensive to feed. As with any commodity when supply outstrips demand, the prices fall and anybody can buy them and usually this leads to impulse purchases. People then keep them in old fish tanks or small, unsuitable enclosures because they don't want to spend the money on a large enclosure. They don't understand these creatures need to climb. They don't want to spend money on light bulbs, so instead they sit them next to a window, a bowl of water is placed in the cage so the chameleon can drink and occasionally a few insects found in the garden. These chameleons then die and instead of the owner looking at themselves and saying "oh I didn't care for it properly" they say "Panther chameleons have a short lifespan".

The biggest killers of Panther chameleons aren't glass enclosures and substrate – it's owners. Ideally, months and months of careful research is needed and experimentation with temperature, humidity and heat is required before buying these creatures. Once bought they still need to be monitored and adjustments need to be made. These are living creatures, yet their lives are cut short because we don't know how to care for them properly.

In short, I think these creatures are wonderful but I also think you need to be prepared for all the time and hard work that goes into them. Be prepared for the wiggly insects running about and making clicking sounds and other insect noises. Be prepared for said insects to escape and run about your house. Be happy to build the perfect habitat and leave your Panther chameleon to enjoy it in peace. In reality, you are investing time and effort into a creature that won't give you a lot back personally – by this I mean you won't get love and cuddles and a pet that rushes to the front of its enclosure, wagging its tail because it's so excited to see you. At best you'll be treated with indifference, at worse you'll be treated in an aggressive manner. However, what you will get is an interesting, beautiful pet and a feeling of contentment as your Panther chameleon thrives and you can watch them bask and eat and go about their lives in a solitary, calm way.